CW01669842

OUT OF THE MOUTH OF THE DRAGON

Mark S. Geston

Mark S. Geston was born in 1946 in Atlantic City, New Jersey, U.S.A. and grew up in Philadelphia. He graduated from Kenyon College, Ohio, with a degree in history. OUT OF THE MOUTH OF THE DRAGON is his second book and the sequel to LORDS OF THE STARSHIP (also available in Sphere Books).

Also by Mark S. Geston and available in Sphere Books

LORDS OF THE STARSHIP

Because God put His adamantine fate
  Between my sullen heart and its desire,
I swore that I would burst the Iron Gate,
  Rise up, and curse Him on His throne of fire.
Earth shuddered at my crown of blasphemy,
  But Love was as a flame about my feet;
  Proud up the Golden Stair I strode; and beat
Thrice on the Gate, and entered with a cry.
All the great courts were quiet in the sun,
  And full of vacant echoes: moss had grown
Over the glassy pavement, and begun
  To creep within the dusty council-halls.
An idle wind blew round an empty throne
  And stirred the heavy curtains on the walls.

Failure
by Rupert Brooke

Out of the Mouth of the Dragon

MARK S. GESTON

SPHERE BOOKS LIMITED
30/32 Gray's Inn Road, London, WC1X 8JL

First published in Great Britain in 1972
by Michael Joseph Ltd.
© 1969 by Mark S. Geston
First Sphere Books edition 1972

TRADE
MARK

Conditions of Sale – This book shall not without the written consent of the Publisher first given be lent, re-sold, hired out or otherwise disposed of by way of trade in any form of binding or cover other than that in which it is published.

The book is published at a net price and is supplied subject to the Publishers Association Standard Conditions of Sale registered under the Restrictive Trade Practices Act, 1956.

Any similarity or apparent connection between the characters in this story and actual persons, whether alive or dead, is purely coincidental.

Printed in Great Britain by
Hazell Watson & Viney Ltd,
Aylesbury, Bucks

"And then I saw three unclean spirits like frogs come out of the mouth of the dragon, and out of the mouth of the beast, and out of the mouth of the false prophet.

"For they are the spirits of devils, working miracles, which go forth unto the kings of the earth of the whole world, to gather them to the battle of that great day of God Almighty.

"And he gathered them together into a place called in the Hebrew tongue, Armageddon."

—REVELATIONS 16: 13, 14, 16

"And I saw the beast and the kings of the earth and their armies, gathered together to make war against him that sat on the horse, and against his army.

"And the beast was taken and with him the false prophet that wrought miracles before him with which he deceived them that had received the mark of the beast, and them that worshiped his image. These both were cast alive into a lake of fire burning with brimstone.

"And the remnant were slain with the sword of him that sat upon the horse, which sword proceeded out of his mouth; and the fowls were filled with their flesh."

—REVELATIONS 19: 19, 20, 21

"And they went up on the breadth of the earth, and compassed the camp of the saints about, and the beloved city: and fire came down from God out of heaven, and devoured them."

—REVELATIONS 20: 9

"And all that was written was accomplished in the fullness of his wisdom and majesty: the captains, their armies, and all of the nations of the earth were encircled with the fire and consumed, even unto ashes and dust.

"But among the ashes and the heaps of dust there lived men that had pledged neither loyalty nor had worshiped him upon the horse or the beast. And in time these men raised upon the land their own nations and appointed their own captains and began to worship, each unto the dictates of his own mind.

"But they were men of ash as were their nations, and little grew upon the land save hatred and frustration. So all lived with the hope of yet another final battle, one where the fire would consume all, and the chasm between the worlds would divide and swallow all, even the ash."

—SURVIVORS 17: 6,7,8

"But again mankind was divided and set upon the plain of Armageddon, although it was called Tynemorgan by the men of Salassar, and again the battle was joined and darkness overthrown by light, and yet again the ashes of battle and the men of ash still lived. And at the sight of them strange wailings were heard beyond the sun; a great sadness swept out of the heart of God and into the soul of the ashen nations. Again, though, the hope of yet another ending helped to turn the ash intc flesh and blood."

—BOOK OF ERIC 2: 37

" 'Who are these men?' he asked me, his face twisted with anxiety. 'They come into our towns and homes and our own brothers become like them, like madmen possessed by ideas which I cannot even begin to fathom. Who are they?' he asked again.

" 'I don't know.'

" 'My own brother!' He railed on, 'He takes one look at that beggar and then it seems like he, he . . . And then that fleet, those ships come and he leaves without a word to me or to his family. God! With ships like those one could rule nations, ransom any throne on earth! But no, he and the others who betrayed us just got on and left. Men who I thought I had known all my life, they turned on me and left. Who are they?'

" 'I don't know.' "

—DIALOGUES OF MORETH, *Chapter IV*

"The battles continue, the last being in memory of my grandfather, breaking and crushing the land into dust compounded; all the Books are erased and many of man's arts have fled his mind.

"There is a thing, a strange melancholy that grows on this world and makes the efforts of men as barren as the soil they are founded upon. Now even the armies that are raised by men to defeat evil fall apart and disintegrate before the battle plain is reached.

"The cancer seems to have invaded more than earth and the hearts of mere men. The clockworks of creation have shorn their gears; stars do not appear at their appointed times; the seasons fail to conform to their immortal standards; and even the surety of a death of pain and damnation begins to seem favorable to the bleeding perversity of earth."

—Inscription on a ruined gate at the Black Library at Iriam, chronology unknown

I

The ship had been badly hurt at the Meadows, and her wounds showed pale yellow and rust in the afternoon sun. Almost a year to the day, she had steamed proudly out of the Goerlin Estuary, eighty of her sisters at either side. There had been battleships afloat on that day, an aircraft carrier, cruisers like herself, and fast destroyers. Now only she remained alive.

All the fading might and wealth and tradition of the Maritime Republics had sailed with that fleet; their flags and the arms of their great houses, all committed to fight on what they judged to be the proper side at the Meadows. By rights, not one should have returned, or even have had a place to return to.

So they had fought, valiantly in many cases, and those empty souls who had chosen to remain behind had seen the night sky burning and felt the ground ripple imperceptibly, even though the Meadows were over two thousand miles away. Surely, if anything could end time and creation, the battle that had erupted upon the Meadows would have done it.

They, the empty people, had found a curious comfort in those days, while the western highlands were edged with red and their china rattled impolitely at teatime. They had even begun to pride themselves in being able to view the situation impartially, free from the passions of those who had embroiled themselves in the struggle. "The plan of creation," wrote Moreth in one of his last Dialogues—how easily he handled such terms, "naturally contains form, content, and a goal at which the first two qualities are aimed. It is further natural that the goal should remain permanently aloof from mortal comprehension; the content is, simply, history; the form, one may safely conclude on the most elementary level, is time. Time is, ultimately, a finite quantity, for if it is divorced from limits, then it ceases to be time and becomes eternity, regardless of how many changes may be contained within it.

"The beginning of time went unrecorded because of the simple absence of observers; but now, at the end, there are observers, men such as myself who feel relief and awe in seeing creation so neatly trimmed off.

"We find relief in that this capstone to time and the universe and all the accompanying phenomena serve finally to illuminate the hand of a true Creator, lying beyond time and mere physical presence. All the brillliant sophistries of dead atheists have fallen before the fulfillment of *Revelations, Survivors,* and the *Book of Eric.* True, these Books have spoken of other battles that were supposed to have ended time, but one can only ascribe poor judgment to their writers, most probably brought on by a feeling of weariness and a disgust with the state of the world.

"But now, we are sure, the final battle is joined, and I have every confidence that those who have committed themselves to the Creator shall carry the day and thus ensure their and their ancestors' salvation.

"I, myself, have not gone to the Meadows. I have, instead, chosen to await the end in my own house, surrounded by my writings and my thoughts. Strange, though I can apparently view the situation with gratifying coolness and objectivity, I could not bring myself to swear allegiance to either side; it could well be that this apathy (that is the wrong word) will be rewarded with eternal damnation. Or it could be that my eldest son, a turret captain on the battleship *Eringold,* may save me (and what of my other two sons? I suspect that they have joined the enemy, but I must not think of that). I have no idea of what shall become of me or of this thing called my soul, and, in the end, I really do not care. Like the authors of *Survivors* and *Eric,* I am tired; I feel that I have long overstayed my time on earth, just as I feel that earth has itself overstayed its proper time."

When the bleeding ship entered the harbor, Moreth drove his sword hilt into the ground and fell upon the blade.

Forty percent of the city's original population had stayed behind, immobilized by confusion or the hopeful emptiness such as had afflicted Moreth. Most of those who had not taken their own lives by that time slowly made their way down to the harbor to see the ship, not to greet her, for they knew that her survival meant that time was to continue and the grinding agony of previous ages would once again be multiplied.

She was named the *Havengore,* after another cruiser which had fought at a previous false-Armageddon; now she was as tragic as her namesake must once have been for they were both, in their time, the lone surviving great ship of once-powerful fleets.

The first *Havengore* had finally contrived to die an honorable death in a battle which, if it did not accomplish all that it was intended to, at least offered an appropriate death to all who fought there. Yet, so disorganized had the battles become that now there were survivors, men and ships even more confused than those who had never gone to the Meadows; they were the ash-men spoken of in *Survivors* and *Eric.* They had heard voices which had instilled in them an absolutely unshakable conviction that *this,* finally, was to be the last act of mankind. They had seen things after which a man had almost no choice but to die. They had fought alongside angels, against demons and devils; and when the noise and smoke had settled, they found themselves alone on the Meadows. The armies had vanished as one would have thought, leaving only their equipment behind to show the survivors there had indeed been a battle. They also left behind pain and despair and hopelessness that was beyond words.

It had taken eight months for the battered cruiser to sail home, dropping off men along the coast, stopping now and then to jury-rig some particularly desperate repairs. She brought five hundred of the Republics' men with her, men who were still trying to decide if they had in some way failed to act in the manner which had been expected of them, or if they had been deserted by their commanders.

She slid past the breakwater at three knots, her twisted and mutilated hull leaving a multitude of small wakes in the quiet water. "B" turret was gone and the bridge immediately behind it had been caved in. The wing of the aircraft which had rammed the ship at that point jutted out over "A" turret, bent and warped from the fires which had welded it to the decks. Three holes of varying diameter could be seen at the waterline; the crane at the stern was bent down until its tip trailed in the water. She was scorched in many places from fires and most of her secondary armament appeared to be out of commission. Two of the seven Republics' flags hung uncertainly at three-quarters mast.

It was very quiet. Not even the sea gulls called any welcome to her; most of them had left with the fleet, a year before. Only silent people, who looked as if they had not slept for months, stared out at the ship and at men who looked distressingly like themselves. The loudest noise was the falling of water as the *Havengore*'s pumps tried to limit the ship's portside list to five degrees.

They all wondered what they should do now. Cry, suicide, accuse someone, anyone? But men could be seen working aboard the cruiser, caring for her, trying to ease her spin; they brought her through the harbor, heading for the shallow water which flanked the mouth of the Goerlin River. The engines were stopped and the remaining anchor let down. By dusk the *Havengore* had settled into the sand on a roughly even keel, the water about ten feet above the waterline.

By noon of the next day they had taken the dead off the cruiser and most of the living; some of her original crew had elected to stay with her, for a while at least.

The shock over the failure of the Meadow War lingered over the city and its reduced population for more than a year. Then, quoting reassuring verses from Scripture or just swearing, the people began to reorganize, giving the city some semblance of its former life.

Aside from the stunted renewal of trade and farming, two great projects came to occupy the city. The first of these was the building of a great cathedral. The predictable reactions to the War's failure would have hardly seemed to have pointed in such a direction, but, with time, as people became accustomed to the world which they were now forced to live in, as they heard even more clearly the wind howling through empty houses and across the lonely earth, they were thrown back upon their initial faith. Perhaps the War would have ended time if they all had gone to the Meadows? Perhaps there were undetected flaws in those who went which prevented a successful conclusion to time?

Besides, when you could bury your life under a slowly growing mosaic proclaiming the glories of the Creator, the taste of your hopes seemed a little less bitter. Eventually some of the men who had seen things which they were sure would cause madness came to look upon those memories as miracles, divine gifts to be treasured for their splendor. The speculations on a failure on the part of the deity grew progressively weaker as the cathedral became a symbol of continuing heavenly favor.

The church was built on top of a small hill, to the west of the city walls. From its steps a road of marble slabs was laid, through the Artillery Gate, where it met the Avenue of Victories with its columns and monuments to ancient battles; then straight down to the harbor and the Sea past the breakwater.

It was quite a splendid road and found a great deal of favor with what still remained of the commercial and landed aristocracy. It became something of a ritual to take one's family out of the city on summer evenings, up to the cathedral to inspect its glacial progress, to comment on some particularly beautiful piece of stained glass which had just arrived from Ihetah-Incalam or wrought iron from New Svald. They stayed there talking with their friends because it was cool and the smells of the inner city could not reach their nostrils. But mostly, they waited for it to get dark, so on walking home, they could not see the dirty, deserted city and harbor.

They seldom visited the harbor anymore and even the briefly revived sea trade soon began to wither. The city became more insulated from the rest of the world, carrying on its chief business within itself, venturing outside only to secure certain luxuries it could not manufacture domestically. The last steel merchantmen had vanished long before the fleet had sailed to the Meadows, but even then a sizable collection of wooden steam and sailing ships had helped to tie the city with such distant points as the Dresau Islands and the crumbling petro-chemical establishments of Cynibal on Blackwoods Bay. Now most of these were gone too, partly because the city's great men no longer saw much reason to journey abroad, and also because the War had effectively removed the old technologies and wealths which had made trade worthwhile. Everywhere in the world, only the merest shadow of what had been remained; and what had been was precious little in the first place.

Aside from the cathedral, the only real activity to be found was at the Old Navy Dock. From there a feeble but steady stream of small boats and rafts sailed the short distance to where the old cruiser was still aground. The reconstruction of the ship was looked upon with a good deal less sympathy than was the cathedral by most of the city. Most of the people who had been to the War remained with the ship as did many of the old sailing men who, although they had not gone to the Meadows, found more comfort in working with armor plate than with glass and ornamental iron. Less than a third of the War's veterans devoted themselves to the new cathedral, but along with them were virtually all of the non-seafaring folk who had stayed home, looking now, perhaps, for a convenient way to prove that they too had found a commitment to the Creator and therefore should not be forgotten when the *real* Armageddon was finally called.

In ten years' time they had laid the foundations and the floor of the nave; the cruiser had also shown much progress and was approaching a marginally seaworthy state, but then only the people directly connected with her really cared. True, there had been a rather ugly confrontation between the aged naval officers who had laid claim to her and the officials of the municipal government who suddenly perceived some advantage in having the only steam-driven, steel warship on the coast (excepting, that is, Enador's two river monitors). The issue was resolved when two five-inch shells landed in front of the cathedral; the only casualty was a draft horse, but the point was made.

The seafarers said they were going back to the Meadows,

if they could find them, to join other stragglers and fight against still more stragglers. The city was glad to be rid of the rusting hulk and her crew of fanatics. In the eleven years since the cruiser had returned, and thus alerted the eastern shorelands of the world to the failure of the War, the messianic, all-consuming faith that had first sent them to the Meadows had become less and less fashionable. Even the memories of what some men had seen faded; eventually they passed from the stage of memory to lapse back into the form of Scriptural allegory, back into the turns of phrase they had worn before assuming concrete form, for a little while, on earth.

The cathedral now not only allowed one to feel a bit less pain—working on the cruiser could do that—but also inspired new thoughts of a reassuringly familiar and distant character. The cruiser would, within the foreseeable future, sail back and try to die again; but the cathedral, with its eternal immovability, its artistry, was comfortably removed from the brutal reality that seemed to keep trying to re-impose its rule over the earth.

It was in the early fall when the great ship staggered past the breakwater, heavy black smoke from low-grade fuel oil pouring from her stacks. There were no flags, no crowds to see her off as there had been twelve years ago. Her existence was quickly forgotten; the city continued its policies of conscious and unconscious contraction, encysting itself from its fellow, similarly encysted city-states, with only the cathedral growing.

The cathedral itself was finished within a hundred years of its beginning, two decades ahead of schedule. Of course, its building had virtually ruined an already frail economy; but at least its magnificence could blind the eye to the decaying walls and buildings of the city, the silted-up harbor, so that now it was no longer necessary to wait until night to go home.

There was a compensation of sorts; the building was quite rightly considered to be an engineering and artistic triumph of its age. From all around the edge of the world came pilgrims traveling to the town for all the endless reasons that force men to undertake such perilous journeys.

So, despite its efforts to insulate itself from the rest of the world, the pilgrims kept the city tied to Enom and Iannarrow, and to the Meadows. According to the wanderers, two calls for Wars in the Meadows had been sent out during the century in which the church was being built. Both had apparently served to end creation only for those who went and the city's populace took a certain smug pride in their having avoided these abortive Armageddons.

But the Wars continued, by now apparently an indistinct series of skirmishes, fed by the survivors of the main battles and by those whom the prophets could still convince that the Millennium was at hand. On occasion, the western horizon flickered red-orange and the votive lamps in the cathedral would swing embarrassingly when there was no draft.

II

Amon VanRoark's father had grown up with the cathedral, first as an apprentice mason, journeyman, and then as a sub-deacon; therefore it was not so very surprising that he turned out a great deal like it, solid, comfortable, absolutely secure in the idea of eternal time. He found it quite easy to ignore the ramblings of disreputable pilgrims and the lamps swinging ever so slightly during mass. The passage of survivors or new men hurrying to the Meadows, the smoke stains of ships below the horizon, even the occasional glitter of silver in the sky and the far rumblings of aircraft high above failed to shake his faith in the rightness of the way things were.

Considering that his wife was of virtually the same mold, it was something of a puzzle that the young VanRoark did not grow up along similar lines. Whether it was the insidious influence of the colony of pilgrims that always surrounded the cathedral, or simply an unusually active imagination, the boy preferred the unknown shadow-lands of the past and its remains. The Old Navy Dock with its ruined factories, the old launches and tugboats awash at their moorings, fascinated him much more than the cool, majestic quiet of the cathedral and its liturgical library. The boy spent too much time on the north side of the harbor and along the banks of the Goerlin River, where still more wrecked shipyards and foundries stood, to be socially acceptable.

The disorganization implicit in the world, with the still-usable remains of advanced technologies existing in the middle of cultures determined to sleepwalk themselves into a standing grave, lent an almost surrealistic air to the world, to VanRoark's eyes at least. It was almost as if time, getting ready to finish its assigned purpose, had somehow gotten fouled up and was now trying desperately to get itself sorted out. When he thought of things like this, a very painful feeling came over him: the feeling of desertion that had first prompted the work on the cruiser and the cathedral.

So usually he just did not think of such matters, content instead to ramble through the ruins, feeling the fine old steel and wondering, always wondering, how it must have been when the night sky still maintained enough regularity by which sailors could navigate.

Spring was late in VanRoark's nineteenth year. As he stood on the cathedral's grand steps and looked down through the Artillery Gate to the harbor, he could see that the ocean was still in its winter mood, heavy chop and spray geysering over the breakwater. He could also see one of the rare trails of smoke rising along the eastern edge of the world.

He stood watching for a while, wondering which way the invisible ship might be heading; but instead of moving off or away the smoke trail grew larger and thicker. By late afternoon a small gray dot could be observed under the column, apparently sailing for the city. VanRoark felt a slight twinge of anticipation, for he had never seen a working steamship. Indeed, his father had said that the last one to visit their harbor had been an armed trawler from New Svald, running from Enador's shore batteries and monitors. Her remains could still be seen, beached on the same flats that the cruiser had briefly rested upon more than a century ago.

He ran into the cathedral to tell his father. When notified

of the approaching ship, he could only say, "Ships have called at our port before, and I am sure they will continue to do so for quite some time. No need to get upset, Amon; if there is any danger to be had from her I am sure that the militia can handle it."

The younger man tried to point out that in its present condition the port offered no reason for merchantmen to call there, and the local forces would be fairly ineffectual against the guns that such an ancient ship probably carried. The elder VanRoark dismissed this with a fatherly smile and said that he must prepare for evening service.

Amon began to mention the Meadow Wars but his father froze him with a glance before the second syllable was out. "Not in the cathedral, not here," he said in a most unfatherly manner.

Amon retreated into the daylight, stumbling down the steps toward the Artillery Gate, more from sudden fear that he may have profaned the sacred precincts than from any burning interest in the ship.

She was only about five miles offshore by then, a rough pillar of gray alternately buried in the gunmetal Sea and then leaping free of it, white spray falling from her bow and decks with a strange delicacy.

The ship was approaching more slowly now with the clouds of vapor shrouding progressively less of her superstructure. A single twin turret, five-inch most probably, was set on the center line directly below the wide bridge; rough shapes, which VanRoark supposed were secondary gun mounts, bristled at odd intervals along her sides.

A mile from the harbor the ship turned to the wind and dropped anchor, apparently not wanting to risk entering an unknown channel with only a few more hours of daylight left. VanRoark supposed that in earlier days she would have been a moderately sized cargo ship, but she was the largest thing that had been seen along the eastern coast of the world for almost half a century. He wondered where she might have come from, from the Dresau Islands or perhaps from islands even farther to the east. And she was old, older even than the cathedral, it seemed. Her sides were streaked with rust and ancient oil. There were no lifeboats in the portside davits which now faced shoreward, although there was a rather sizable launch secured on the afterdeck, tied to the only remaining cargo crane. She had never been designed to take any armament, but in addition to the forward twin turret, duplicated aft, at least three large gun tubs could be made out on the facing side, their contents hidden under huge, dirty tarpaulins.

But the lines were still there under the dirt and the crudely welded repair sheets: the graceful curve and flare of the bows, the long waterline leading back to a short, cut-off stern; a low, beautifully terraced superstructure set well aft. VanRoark, quite surprising himself, thought that she was much too fine to still be afloat; she should have died along with the world that built her.

Dinner was an unusually tense affair for both of the elder VanRoarks, along with most of the city's population, who were determined not to acknowledge the ship's presence, even though her lights were clearly visible from every vantage point. The absence of any hostile action from her, in most minds, removed any cause for concern about her existence. However, if the crew wished to purchase any provisions, that was another matter.

The young man became more distressed with himself as the evening went on. Before, he could easily observe and speculate over dead and harmless places like the Old Navy Dock, its tiny, rotting fleet of sunken ships, and the illegible inscriptions on the monuments along the Avenue of Victories. Now these thoughts were intruding dangerously close to a full awareness; true, they could easily be nothing but fragments of truth, blown way out of proportion by his notorious imagination, but the refusal of anyone to discuss them, even on the most superficial level, only served to magnify them once again. His own speculations began to expand and connect themselves with childhood stories and legends told by pilgrims on the cathedral's steps; the ruins which had always been taken as a normal part of the city suddenly began to seem vaguely extraordinary.

His bedroom was on the third story of the VanRoark home (cathedral officials being among the better paid of the city's population). Unfortunately, it overlooked the bay and the ship's lights. The night sky was darkly thick with stars, and such a curious feeling it was to look down and see yet another constellation where the Sea should have been, until the rocking of the ship separated its lights from the welkin's. Electric lights. VanRoark guessed at this just as he was about to drowse off to sleep; electric lights had left the city along with the old cruiser a hundred years before. How cold they burned, so cold and silver . . . not with the nice, red flickering of the animal fur lamps used nowadays.

Around four o'clock the false dawn appeared, restoring the mere physical presence of the ship. As VanRoark finally fell to sleep he began to sense a movement that flowed westward from the Sea and the ship, through the city and, ultimately, to the Meadows. It was a completely insubstantial movement, and as far as the city was concerned a limited and retrogressive one. But the feeling was a tremendously perplexing and upsetting one, for it unavoidably displaced the static security of his education, his society, and the cathedral. Very slowly, VanRoark was beginning to rebuild within himself a sense of time and a sense of history, concepts which like the old ships and the electric lights had long ago departed from the world.

III

The young VanRoark had been apprenticed to one of the cartography firms still left in the city; it was something of a wonder that even these few had any business considering that not many people had use for maps. So, more and more, the chartmakers had turned to fancy and imagination, producing works of great artistic beauty but with only the most superficial claims to accuracy.

It was in his shop, seated before the old desk at the back and gazing continually at the old portfolios, where VanRoark had accumulated much of his latent store of bewilderment with his own home. How fascinating it was to trace the old maps, so yellowed and eaten through with worms, and then compare them with those of more recent vintage. Small wonder that the mapmakers had given up the real world in disgust, for even the ancient, seemingly exact maps showed monstrous discrepancies even within the space of several decades: the magnetic field of the earth had reversed itself at least twice in the past three centuries. VanRoark further came to the conclusion that the night sky over his home bore little resemblance to that which had existed even in the time of his father's youth.

He had chosen a roundabout way of going to the shop so that he could avoid any sight of the roadstead. But his mind was still unaccountably afire and it was useless to try to eat lunch; at noon, VanRoark gave in to himself and walked down Bergman Street to Admiralty Square along the harbor.

The old Square had once been a center of municipal life—a function now fulfilled by the cathedral—when the city still owed allegiance to the Sea. Weeds now poked between the marble paving blocks and even the great monumental column to the city's lost ships and sailors was cracked and tinged with blue-green mosses. Despite the low-tide stench that grew stronger as the harbor gradually turned itself into a swamp, it was still something of a gathering place; many of the poorer classes who did not feel entirely comfortable amidst the ornate splendor of the cathedral gardens, along with the old naval families whose heritage was tied only to the Sea, came to sun themselves and let the living Sea remind them that all was not yet dead or dying in the world.

VanRoark walked into the Square, briefly eyeing the anonymous captain who still looked seaward from atop the column, four seadragons guarding his high pedestal; then his eyes moved to the Sea, where the ship rode at anchor. But his attention was ripped back to the old docks that started at the southern end of the Square and then ran down to the commercial districts. A new craft was moored there and VanRoark guessed that it was the launch he had seen on the ship's afterdeck.

He moved toward it and would have broken into a dead

run had he not been afraid it should turn out to be just another one of the infrequent hulks that still called at the port. It had to be the ship's; motor-driven, its lines resembled nothing he had ever seen except along the margins of old maps. She was very sharp, only about seventy feet long and obviously built for speed. VanRoark stared in deeper fascination as he realized the ship was in excellent shape and entirely free of rust; in the few spots where her gray and black colors had been chipped only the fresh silver of untouched metal showed through. There were no guns, not even any mounts or other signs that she had ever carried anything else but power; never had he seen anything so full of latent energy, and he could feel his mind being pulled along in her wake, splitting through the fragile, rotten immovability of the city.

The implied movement of the ship drew him back to the Square; a figure had mounted one of the seadragons. A group of sailors stood at its feet, waiting.

He was a rather tall fellow, probably thin for his height, but the shapeless robes he wore hid most of his build. VanRoark could see his face, even though he was still far away; he could see the eyes burning and glittering like gas torches. Loose brown hair fell from his head and down his back. But his eyes!

VanRoark tumbled forward, quite unaware of what he was doing or that others had joined him. He sensed another feeling growing within him, something far beyond those which the ships had conjured; so fantastically complex and alien it was, that it lost and blurred itself with its twistings and infinite surfaces. All he could really define was a shortness of breath and loss of balance, as if he were walking along the edge of a cliff with nothing but fog below him.

He stopped before the monument. He knew who the man was. Then a name, Timonias, drifted through the mob. Timonias. Vision became indistinct, especially along the outer edges of his sight. The gray-green of steps and seadragons seemed to merge with the brilliant white of Timonias' robes, moving slightly in the breeze. Words and thoughts flickered and turned outside VanRoark's suddenly narrowed world; only one voice and one idea and one person could now penetrate him. He had anchored his moment to the face and eyes and hands of Timonias; he did not have the slightest idea who Timonias was, but he knew him.

Then the hand, more pale than the robe around it, moved up before the diamond eyes and VanRoark was swept along. Never could he have conceived of a voice such as the one the man on the seadragon had: one that spoke, it seemed, without words or sound. The movement which all speakers seek to propel into the minds of their listeners was now existing as a force alive in itself.

Dust, and then from it, stars and planets; diagrams of creation unrolled in the space between Timonias' eyes and his weaving hand. Then history, a thing which VanRoark had been gradually resurrecting within himself over his few years, came to his reeling mind, bludgeoning it back and forth against the limits of time.

He heard nothing, he was fairly sure of that; but like the name of the man atop the seadragon, the knowledge came to him, emerging and twisting within a consciousness that was unable to close and permanently grasp it—only to remotely observe it and attempt the frail lash-ups of memory.

Battles, cities, the conquest of the stars and then a retreat; spinning violence and the cool, grinding tragedy of things which he forgot even as they came to him flowed around the world of Admiralty Square. Rise and fall, bleeding defeat and stupid rebirth: things *passed* by him, and it came driving home that the wrecks had not always lain along the Goerlin's mud flats, that there had not *always* been ruins upon the earth. This he remembered; and because of this, some small, distant part of him sent up a terrible wailing and a sorrow he thought impossible to surpass.

Timonias was still speaking; the wailings died, the sorrow quickly calloused itself against any feeling. Now the pace rose and became even more fantastic; like the burning of blue diamonds and deep opals the "words" spun and sparkled far beyond the hand and eyes of the prophet, far beyond the tragicomic procession that had just bulleted through VanRoark's mind. Now came the final hope, the promise of peace and an ending, a truly brilliant, truly inspired end to the construct of the universe.

For a second, VanRoark drew back, awed and perversely proud of the neatly finished-off picture, the wonderfully complete aspect which time and history had suddenly attained from the words and gestures of Timonias.

Then the thoughts paled and turned to sand to drift away. Only a few grains were left . . . but they were enough.

IV

VanRoark slowly regained his vision; his mind closed back upon itself to find the small fragments that remained. Timonias had gone, as had the sailors and the motor launch. The ship was still anchored about a mile offshore, but the thick stream of smoke that hung above her showed she would be leaving soon too.

He was standing where he had been, before the sea-dragons and dead captain; but it was almost sunset now and the Square was utterly deserted. Long shadows from deserted buildings and ruins formed a tracery across the stones and around the monument.

Far away the shining towers of the cathedral could be seen, the crosses and stars at their peaks gouging the bloated sun. VanRoark wondered how long he had been standing there; if, indeed, this was the same day or year that he last remembered. There was nothing inside him now that he could articulate; not a single concept had remained in any recognizable form. But the ideas had passed through him brutally, and the small waves from their dying wake stirred inside him, much more in his heart and stomach than in his mind.

So it was with no small wonderment at his own behavior that he wandered through the dead streets, trying to dig down through their tumbling masses and recapture them for rational examination. Back up to Bergman Street, past the shuttered cartography shop, and under the wooden compasses and globes that marked the other shops along the street; most of them had closed down years ago and the weathered signs, decayed and falling to pieces, described the measurements of the street and its new ruins with their shadows.

VanRoark stopped and tried to restore a hanging basket-work globe to its mount; but the iron thorns that had once held metal continents to the framework, now probably melted down for the cathedral, cut his fingers.

The sun was down; a brilliantly moonless welkin recast the weathered wood and ulcerated paint into a vague parody of steel or silver. VanRoark moved on across the Avenue of Victories; dry fountains spouted stars and hideous new constellations. Then the feelings he had been attempting to grasp began to rise to his mind; he was instantly terrified. Echoes of his wailing and sorrow came piling back upon him, the things Timonias had told following behind. He ran from the Avenue of Victories and the cathedral, leaving the night sky twisting with the quiet agony of a dumb animal.

V

Amon VanRoark found a distant amusement with himself in the day immediately following the appearance of Timonias. Somewhere, still miraculously untouched, a bit of himself which cared nothing for matters of such great import as the end of time hung back to watch the curious activities of the rest of him. It was not, in any way, irritation or resistance to the new course of VanRoark's life. But as he blundered about his room—absurdly trying to decide just what he should take with him to the Meadows and the presumed presence of God—the small bit asked why the streets were not awash with men desperate to get out of the city and join the armies of their true nature.

Indeed, the city seemed completely normal, perhaps even intensely normal, as if it were trying to ignore the extraordinary happenings of the previous day. The usual apathy of most people seemed to suddenly require more effort than usual. The pack of drifters and derelicts who were always sleeping in the ruins around the Artillery Gate squirmed uneasily, with their eyes screwed shut as if a brilliant light had been thrust in front of them. Everywhere the failure and futility which had served to carry so many of the city's generations safely through life no longer appeared to be so natural a thing.

Clearly the city had been touched, but as VanRoark walked about on the day before he planned to leave for New Svald he heard not a word of the two ships or the prophet or anything being the slightest bit uncommon. *Perhaps,* he thought for a moment, *each man is now fighting his own battle, trying to decide whether to throw his lot in with Good or Evil; in a day or two the city will erupt into activity. Companies will be raised, final alliances formed, the promises fulfilled.*

Because of this, VanRoark delayed his departure for a few more days, then a week. Instead of exploding, the city merely closed itself up tighter, driving whatever thoughts that had briefly stirred it deeper and deeper into its routine until they were finally lost. Two weeks after Timonias had visited the city, VanRoark could almost feel the pressure being released. They had entirely defeated the thing that now so possessed the young man, beaten and smothered it until it became just one more of the small, vague irritations that had come to make up what passed for a heritage in those days.

While the city met and easily dealt with the Word, VanRoark only surrendered to it. He began to fear that the Meadow Wars might somehow begin without him. He had tried to talk to his father about Timonias but was met with such determined inattention that he soon gave up. This bothered him intensely. Hostility, anger: at least they were positive and would mean that the elder VanRoark, too, was taking sides. But this nothingness: "Did you see him, Father, or have your men told you about him and what he said? Did you see the ships? The small, fast one and the big, tired one anchored offshore?" Somehow the conversation always managed to return to such subjects as the impending Feast of

St. Mathiason, or the eternal plans of the City Council to begin deepening the harbor, now little more than a marsh.

A small, cold rage began to build up within VanRoark, which made him want to scream what he had heard to every citizen he could reach. But the rage never grew to be very large, simply because he was much too caught up in his own personal adventure to really care much for the trials or failings of others. Besides, he knew perfectly well that it was impossible for him to ever tell another person what he knew; only Timonias could do that and he had gone.

Although the prophet had never stated such, VanRoark anticipated a brave, grimly happy air on the day he would leave, for he expected, on that day, to have the rest of the city marching with him. *Lord,* he thought, *this should be a time for grand farewells and beau gestes of impossible charm; flags should be flown; people who were enemies to the very centers of their souls should be making one last wish for luck and good fortune to each other.*

Instead, he stood alone by the Artillery Gate, damp from the early morning mists and uncomfortable from the suspicious stares of a couple of derelicts. Behind him was the great cathedral, soft and shadowy in the fog, small rays of colored light hovering around the stained glass windows; the lamps had not swayed for more than ten years. Ahead of him, the Avenue of Victories, its ruins and civic tombstones gradually vanishing in the mist; he could see nothing of the harbor.

He had thought briefly of saying goodbye to some people, especially a woman he knew in the Thurber District—a place of moldering buildings that had once housed the various legations and embassies to the city, when nations still thought contact with the rest of the world to be, if not necessary, then at least gentlemanly. The quarter was known for its eccentrics and odd characters; certainly she was one of the strangest, and one of the most enchanting, of all who lived there. But he knew if he went, it would only be with the secret hope that he might impress her with his plans, and that she, in turn, would somehow dispel the knowledge that was driving him away. He remembered his absolute inability to communicate what he knew to anyone, even to her; and if she already knew, then she had most probably left anyway.

He had not said goodbye to either his mother or father, St. Mathiason having laid a momentary claim to their attentions, and he cared little for the other people he knew in the city. But the girl, that was a real hurt. Small and distant, like the part of him that was so amazed by his actions, she could not change his course, but he wondered if she might have been at Admiralty Square and if she, too, was going to the Meadows; he wondered which side she would be on.

He stood looking at his city until the mists had burned off, hoping that it might suddenly break out of itself and join him. Nothing happened, nothing unusual stirred the warm, damp air. At least he would be leaving in a proper spring instead of the odd winter that had stayed with the land into the middle of May.

In other times—when the Avenue of Victories had not stopped at the steps of the cathedral but had run straight west for more than a thousand miles, through the Great Plains and to the nation of Timmerion—there had been an exceptionally fertile strip of land which had roughly paralleled the coast from the Republics south to the Talbight Estuary. It had been called the Greenbelt, and upon its soil the Republics had raised their most beautiful flowers, grown their greatest crops, bred their finest horses. But the endless wars and catastrophes had crushed and poisoned the Greenbelt into a near-desert, even more barren now than the land which surrounded it. In winter it was frozen to the hardness of metal; in the summer, if the season chose to ever arrive, it would be dust; nothing but ironbush and saltgrasses could grow there.

Now it was spring and the Greenbelt was muck; it clung and stuck to VanRoark's boots and made him feel filthy. But his only alternative was the endless lands to the west, where it was only a matter of chance if he would be murdered before or after he got lost.

VI

VanRoark's luck improved momentarily; four days out from his city, he fell in with a caravan of adventurers from the lands of Raud. They were going south also, but to the vast Enstrich Marshes to hunt for bird-of-paradise feathers and the hides of the water reptiles that lived there; a curious sort of crystal grew in pockets along the reptiles' bodies that was highly prized among certain rulers and noblemen, especially those of the mountain kingdoms of Mountjoy and ancient Mourne. None of them had ever heard of any Timonias, and it was absolutely impossible to draw them into conversation about anything other than women, feats of drinking, or the vast sums they planned to make from their enterprise.

VanRoark was quite aware that he should be getting more dispirited over the absence of fellow travelers to the Wars; on several occasions, when the dubious security and small comforts of home grew large through comparison to the caravan's meager offerings or, at night, when he thought of the woman he had never said goodbye to, a purely pitiful human crying took hold of him. He felt so very old and tired for his age, and the part of him that remained cynically amused observed that even the possessed must still remain essentially human.

That thought pained him: that he should still feel hunger and loneliness and longing. But most of the time, and always in the daylight, the words of Timonias stayed with him, pushing him on.

Gradually the landscape became flatter and the low hills bordering the western horizon leveled off. At times, when the air was exceptionally clear, a gray-green edging of far highlands could be seen. The coastline remained quite rugged, cliffs dropping vertically a hundred feet or more to the Sea.

The Trextel River, which began among the same lake system as the wilder Shirka, emptied into the Sea through an impressive fjord that ran almost a hundred miles eastward. At its real mouth, far inland, there had once been a great trading city, whose ruins were still something of a marvel to those who visited them. Its name is not remembered, but the fortress town of Charhampton, which had guarded the seaward mouth of the gorge, remained. The city and its attendant forts had been carved into the rock sides of the northern cliffs. It had long been a strong point and its scars, everything from the chips made by steel axes to the shadow-impressions of people caught by a bomb that had once exploded in the gorge, attested to its importance.

The trade that had made the city important had vanished centuries ago, or else shifted to Enador, but a few people still managed to extract a living from the Sea or from selling the scrap metal and armaments from the dead forts. The caravan stopped to rest at Charhampton and to wait for the ferry that would take them to the southern bank of the Trextel. The lizard hunters retired to the bars and single whorehouse of the city for the evening; VanRoark might have joined them, but puritan tinges of his upbringing held him back. Overshadowing that was the prospect of exploring the ruined forts, whose galleries and quays ran for nearly a mile downstream from the city until they curved north along with the coastline as it opened to the Sea.

Most of the smaller structures and miscellaneous junk had been carted away and probably remounted in castles from North Cape to Enom. The forts of Charhampton, though, like the fabled Armories of which little remained except for a few caves and a crater on the Tyne River, had been built by a mighty nation of men who could bend almost anything, but their own minds, to their will. Thus, great and incomprehensible machines remained, rooted to their concrete bases, still pointing across the river or seaward through slits in the rock.

He had been wandering through some ancient submarine pens about a quarter of a mile east from the city itself, when he met Tapp. Tapp was, of course, fairly drunk, a state which he successfully maintained for almost the whole time

VanRoark knew him. The young man was quite startled, lost as he was in the dreams and nightmares that the rusting hulks inevitably conjured.

"Good evening, young sir. In search of your new command?" Tapp's deep voice bellowed through the huge pens. VanRoark quickly picked out the little man sitting atop the conning tower of one of the near boats. Tapp gestured grandly at the ragged patchwork of ribs and hull plating.

"And are you to be my crew?" VanRoark responded after a moment.

"Aye, sir, if it pleases you. But I fear that our ships will need a bit of work before we sail." Tapp burst into sudden, explosive laughter at his own wit. Fascinated, VanRoark drew closer, more than a little amazed at his own fearlessness, for he had long been taught of the creatures that were said to lurk in the remains of the dead world.

"And for where shall we be sailing, crew? For Blackwoods Bay, Duncarin or the Isle of Oromund?" VanRoark knew perfectly well the place he hoped the man would name.

A pause while the laughing echoed out to Sea through the ruined blast doors and torpedo booms. "Why, to the Meadow Wars, young sir!" Then, even lower and more sadly, "To the Meadows . . ." But again the quiet pens detonated to his laughter; he reached behind him and drew out a short, curved saber that caught moonlight reflected from the water outside and from the shell holes in the roof. "Right, young sir, to the bleeding Meadows, you know. Like my great-grandfather, like my granddad, and my own dad. The other two came back, but old Dad pulled it off and managed to die when he was supposed to." He lowered the saber, bent over and lifted a wine sack from inside of the old conning tower. "Juice?" he asked with momentary politeness; and then back up with the sword and his voice filling the pens. A colony of bats stirred into the air and then nested again in another corner. VanRoark said no, but was this a joke or was he really going to the Meadows?

"Joke indeed! The only bleeding joke around here is . . . is" —he fumbled thickly for the proper words—"is that we are here." Satisfied that his point had been made, he took another pull on the sack and flourished his saber in the wet air. Then his voice fell again. "You know, young sir?" He looked up abruptly. "Your name, if I may be so forward?"

"Amon VanRoark." The youth bowed slightly to the drunk. "And yours?"

"Second Lieutenant Tapp, lately of the kingdom of Cynibal and servant of his Imperial Majesty, Bournmouth the Third, Conqueror of Worlds, Liege of Creations. Also lately running from charges of treason relating to the disappearance of the steam frigate *Toriman* and its subsequent reappearance under the flag of the free city of Enador." He drank again from the leather sack, smacking his lips with delight at the foul brew. "And also, my sir, a wanderer, a man of vast passions and laughter and loneliness." Now his voice was soft and dreamy, as if he fancied himself possessed of a poetic soul. Impressed with his own depth of feeling, he lost the thread of his conversation. "Where was I, sir?" he blurred at VanRoark.

"You were Tapp, man of vast—"

"Ah yes, that Tapp. Indeed I was . . . am. You see, I am a wanderer, I've seen many nations, and none of them, and heard at my mother's side the tale of my father marching to the Meadows with all the lads of great Cynibal beside him. And how he never came back, and how, in some way I *still* cannot understand, I should be happy for him in that."

A curious shade of water-reflected silver and shadow crossed over his rutted face, drawing VanRoark nearer, quite against his better nature. Then the little man sighed again and set his voice into a new, solemn tone. "And then, you see, sir, ten years ago a man came to Cynibal all dressed in fine white. And he spoke to us, to me, and he said there was going to be a war at a place called the Meadows, and how, if we wanted to save our souls, we had to go and fight there. Now, young sir, I remembered perfectly well that three of my forebears had set off on just such a venture, probably even heard the same things and had the same hopes. But I had never *heard* the men who had spoken to them. And though I knew all this, I also knew beyond all doubt that *this* would be our last gesture in time.

"So I ditched my commission, which was getting a little

hot anyway from the *Toriman* row, and left my bawling old lady and several other broken hearts, to travel west with some fellow lunatics. It took about a year, overland and by Sea, but at last we made it to a place called the Burn. It's a very old place, you know, and I was told that one of the false-Armageddons had been fought there. Ghastly place, sir, all burned and blasted, and the mountains look like they had been melted once. You think the Belt is dead? It's a flaming paradise compared to the Burn. Lord," he muttered, shaking his head and taking a drink, "a flaming paradise.

"But there were others like me there, a whole bleeding army! All come to do old Evil and Time their last." Then, even more slowly, "And, sir, when we marched from the Burn to the Meadows you could *feel*, sir, you could *feel* God moving with us! Two million men maybe—I don't know just how many—and all around us there were . . . were . . ." He began fumbling again, trying to pull thoughts and memories from places his mind had hidden them in, lest they run wild, raging about and turning the sane parts of him rotten. ". . . lights, moving lights . . . and creases of shadow floating around us, but we could still feel them pressing in on us. God! How powerful we felt, so bleeding full of Right and Good and all the . . . Godddd, sir!" Tapp yelled, low and savage. "They were there! The whole bleeding lot of them, sir! I saw them!" He slammed his fists into his eyes and began moaning, only bothering to make the curses understandable.

VanRoark wanted to leave, for he was at once terrified and embarrassed by the man; but he stayed and after a while the man was quiet, put the saber into its scabbard and threw the empty wine skin into the stagnant water. VanRoark rose and helped the little man descend the conning tower; his hands were cut by the rusted metal and the red flowed darkly into the saliva Tapp had drooled onto them. He began mumbling apologies to both VanRoark and God, begging VanRoark to take him away from the pens to a nice dry gutter where he might sleep it off.

Moved by the knowledge that here at last was a man who had been to the Meadows and, more importantly, was journeying back there again, VanRoark dragged him back to the cut-rock streets of Charhampton and dropped him into a room which the inn's landlord had thoughtfully provided for drunken members of the caravan. He left the man snoring peacefully, but later that night, when the house was awakened by screaming, he knew that it was Tapp; VanRoark dared not move from his bed or open his eyes until another drunk had silenced him.

VII

They crossed the Trextel River the next day and continued southward between the Greenbelt and the somewhat less rugged coastline. Tapp had joined them.

It took them two months of traveling to reach Enador, on the south bank of the Talbight Estuary. The traveling was relatively pleasant, or as pleasant as their world would allow it to be. Tapp, being almost continually drunk, did very little to maintain the company, but from him streamed an incredible succession of lies and legends, stories ranging from amazingly accurate recitations from Cynibal's treasure books to equally amazing tales of virility in her brothels. His grand gestures and inflated oratory easily caught the ears of the young men from Raud, with their own dreams of piety and pornography, so Tapp was never without enough liquor to fuel his memory. VanRoark did not question him about the Wars again, much as he would have liked to, for he feared it would break the mood of their traveling as they followed the end of summer south.

Besides a growing affection for this man with the deep olive skin and jaundiced eyes, there arose another feeling in VanRoark. For so long he had been empty, content only to gather small bits of a dubious past and to move through his existence with little real trouble or thought. Then he had fatally begun to assemble the old fragments into understandable patterns, patterns which the "words" of Timonias had blasted into a picture of history.

But this was a scar and did nothing to fill up his merely earthly existence. Now he began to surround it with conceptions of life such as he had never come to before. Always to his left was the Sea, bright and glittering and forever restless. To his right, the Greenbelt with its dust and poisons and the gunmetal mountains behind it: always dead, eternal, unmoving, except to crumble into finer dust. The Sea was just as eternal, but its timelessness was one of life, not death. How curious that he had never really noticed the life teeming in the Sea, the flying fish and dolphin that cut through its surface and flew over it, the white of its surf and beaches. He looked to the Greenbelt and saw its diseased ironbushes and saltgrasses, a large wolf spider eating another wolf spider.

Once, when they had camped on the straits that separated the mainland from the Isle of Oromund, he had walked out onto the sterile expanse of the Belt. It was dusk, the only time of day that the land acquired anything faintly resembling beauty, a desolate lunar beauty. He stopped and in the half-light spotted a brilliantly colored bug by his foot; most of the Belt's inhabitants were either a dirty tan or dun color, but this one was garishly marked in turquoise and yellow stripes, its legs booted in white and a hood of the same color running up its many-jointed neck and mantis head. VanRoark bent down to examine the creature, and then walked quickly back to the camp, much sicker than he thought he should have been.

The cannibalism of the wolf spiders was to be expected in such a detestable looking breed. But the wondrously colored bug had twisted its long neck over its body and was calmly, methodically disemboweling itself; the opal wings were easily spread so that its jaws might reach its vitals sooner. It was the careful, infinitely methodical feeling of the self-dissection that bothered VanRoark; trapped on the world, or at least ignorant of the Sea, the insect was committing suicide, an act that either implied intelligence in a very primitive life form, or merely the dictate of instinct. It was this last thought and its implications that drove him back to the Sea and Oromund's shadowed hills.

The Sea, though, was always full with that which lived and moved and functioned and was clean. There, life was not scarred from radiation or dying from birth because of disease or starvation; nowhere else on the earth did such life exist, and as VanRoark walked beside it, saw its storms for the first time beating upon its own washed beaches, instead of silted, filth-clogged harbors, his spirits rose. The Wars faded and cooled in him; he kept traveling only because of the Sea and because there was no reason at all to return home.

VIII

VanRoark did not find out that Tapp was dying until they had reached Enador. The weapons that had been used at the Meadows by some men, while not fatal, had given him radiation poisoning. He had lived through the initial dose as he had through the Wars themselves, but it had left behind a small unpredictable cancer. The only outward manifestation of it, aside from the pain and the vomiting of blood, was a bleeding ulcer on the back of Tapp's neck. It had briefly flared after the Meadows, and then subsided, only seasonal fluctuations and the lightly stained collars reminding him of its presence. Now it had grown, round and angry, dribbling pus and reddened lymph down his neck. Tapp took this to be an indication of his impending end; thus the liquor, and the journeying to the Meadows—again.

VanRoark found a richness in the tangle of Tapp's motives such as he had seldom seen in the world. Why was he going to the Meadows? he would ask again when Tapp was sober. And in time Tapp said that he was going to avenge his father's death, to find glory, or booty, or make his death a bit less painful than the doctors had prophesied, or to fight in a holy war, a jihad that had been declared against a human enemy and not creation. Of course, beyond all of this lay the things he had said and remembered in the submarine pens, things that still managed to creep out of their hiding places for a moment to turn his eyes to the ground and to make his hands pick nervously at the bleeding wound in his neck.

He seemed to like the jihad fiction the best, for he could play up an equally false cynicism against it. "Right, then, Roark," he would sometimes command, his saber in his right hand and the other clamped upon VanRoark's shoulder, "off to the Meadows to fight for the Prophets with their glittering eyes, and thousands of the Faithful behind us! Ah, grand it'll be, us sweeping the Infidel before us, circumcising them on the run!"

Van Roark would support him with questions of the spires, harems, and other attendant treasures that would fall to them once the Meadows were crossed and the unknown lands north of them captured. He still feared to let Tapp slide down into his memories, yet half hoping that he would.

IX

They stayed at Enador for a week, waiting for a ship to carry them south; the rather doubtful location of their destination didn't trouble them much. Although when they inquired at chandleries, cartography shops, or along the waterfront, they got either a rough laugh, a glob of spit at their feet (at which Tapp's ulcer would blaze deep scarlet and his hand would start moving for the saber's pommel), or a patronizing smile. At least people had heard of the Meadows.

Enador was still one of the few places left on the eastern coast of the world that could still lay any claim to wealth or power; chiefly, her riches came from the Sea, upon which she still carried a reasonably active commerce, and her slow cannibalization of the remains of the Dresau Islands. The Islands had died soon after they had sent their last fleet to fight at one of the false-Armageddons; but her sailors had left a lot behind and now only Enador had the ships and the desire to pick the bones. The two river monitors which allowed Enador to control the Talbight Estuary all the way to Donnigol were armed with Dresau guns, powered by Dresau engines, and fueled with oil that had lain in storage tanks outside of Duncarin for centuries.

But even so, Enador's stance was as precarious as any in the world, perhaps more so in view of the land and sea areas she aspired to control. Too often were the monitors lobbing shells into the rebellious primitives of Svald or Lairne when the lizards and hooded basilisks from the Enstrich Marshes swam or crawled north and their eyes could be seen from the city's walls.

Regardless of all this, Enador was still the trading center of the known world, and as such she almost always had a fair amount of commerce in her roadstead and harbor. VanRoark noted that many of the ships were scavengers, dealing in the remains of worlds long dead, like those that brought the guns and sheet steel from the Dresau Islands, the fortresses of Charhampton and the Armories.

As the world drank more and more blood from the bodies of its predecessors and gnawed more deeply into their putrefied flesh, the scavenger ships were forced to sail farther outward, to the fjords and bays of the anonymous northlands or to the Old Nations to the west and south past Ihetah-Incalam. VanRoark and Tapp left the party of hunters and began looking for ships journeying to such far points.

Inside a week they had paid passage on a barque of two thousand tons, the *Garnet;* her master was going to the Meadows, as were they, because of the calling of the prophet. But he reckoned no further than the concentration of military equipment that would surely be found there. A light-fingered crew of sufficient delicacy would be able to garner a rich harvest of small arms and explosives before the Holy became wise. And, who knows, they were sailing to a place of great tradition and antiquity; even if no army was being gathered there, the place should offer more than enough in salvageable material to make the voyage highly profitable.

So they sailed on board the *Garnet* with her mob of

greedy half-wits and two others who were merely half-wits, in Tapp's initial judgment. The first, a tall emaciated man named Yarrow, who spent most of the voyage spitting his rotting lungs over the side, was an undiluted fanatic; he delighted at spouting Scripture from any one of a hundred holy books and prophesying a glorious end for the four of them. VanRoark knew that his words were taken with fair accuracy from the very same books which had been Timonias' silent and neglected forerunners; but to hear the grand words clothed in Yarrow's grandiloquent and affected posturing, his theatrical tone, destroyed for the moment all the grimly wonderful completeness of the Meadows. What was supposed to happen there was reduced to a sordid collection of meaningless gestures. Both Tapp and VanRoark avoided this man and let him vent his righteous furies upon the crew.

The other man, Gerideau Smythe, was also a fanatic, or at least he tried to make one believe he was. But somehow his quiet, calm assertions of faith and belief and ain't-we-gonna-stick-it-to-ole-Satan-pass-the-Lord-and-praise-the-ammunition simply could not come off with the same loud, utterly blind conviction with which Yarrow could fill them. Neither did he have the immovable but strangely shrouded convictions that seemed to be driving VanRoark to the Meadows.

He had been a librarian by profession—which meant that half the nations in the world had laws by which he could be legally murdered—first at the Black Library at Krysale Abbey and then at the more notorious one at Iriam. Thus he had grown up among the works which proved that this world had been preceded by another, and that by another, and so forth, until the old maps VanRoark had wondered at found histories to match their mountains and rivers. Of course, to be a librarian in those days only meant that one had to be reasonably literate; but there must have been a devotion in Smythe that tied him so closely to the books he could read but never fully understand.

At night when Yarrow had preached the dolphins into a sleepy stupor and Tapp had predictably passed out, Smythe would talk to VanRoark of the great, fortress-like libraries and recite fragments and pieces of histories and sciences that had randomly stuck in his mind; virtually all of the names were foreign to VanRoark, so many Republics Of and Unions Of. Not at all like the present, when nations drew their names from their dead founders—or their assassins.

It was not at all hard, when his mind was already awash with Tapp's magnificent blitherings, to listen to Smythe's cracked voice, for he was an old man now, and after a while the pious trappings would slough off and the wonder that the libraries had sheltered began to fearfully poke through. It would only be for a few minutes, a half hour at the most, before the guilt that stood behind the religious and moral slogans drove the glittering shapes back; but for the instant they lived.

In the darkness the dreadful state of the *Garnet* was invisible and, with the sordid mumblings of her crew ended for the day, there existed only VanRoark and the Sea and Smythe's voice. VanRoark learned of air ships from the old man, and how the steel ships were able to propel themselves without sails or paddle-wheels; how the old, vanished cities used to look, and how they died, quickly under the bombs, or slowly at their own hands as gangs of kids stuffed homemade guncotton and broken glass into oatmeal cans and let their parents bleed to death on sidewalks; he learned of asphalt roads that had once covered the world, and of the vehicles that had carried men upon them; ships that dived into the sea, and ships that had carried other men on some few faltering steps toward the stars, before there was no more time for such things.

It was, of course, for these things that the man was truly going to the Meadows; even VanRoark came to see that. But somehow, someone had convinced Smythe that the knowledge he had watched over was the very essence of evil, of the dark, power-ravening evil that man had allowed to grow within himself in his younger years. Now, as Yarrow believed, such things were behind him and all man needed was a clean heart and mind averted exclusively toward Heaven. Poor Smythe tried so desperately to ape Yarrow's florid statements of faith, but he was a bad liar and the libraries at Krysale Abbey and Iriam were still very much with him. He had burned Krysale, or rather had been forced to by a group heading for one of the Meadow's unending Wars.

It was in these conversations with Smythe that VanRoark first began to question his own motives for going to the Meadows. The time of Timonias still had that beautifully rounded-off character that fairly screamed for completion, his head was still quite full of the things he had sensed at Admiralty Square, but now, as the stars above the horizon appeared as the running lights of great battle fleets, he finally admitted to himself an entirely heretical and apparently irrelevant love of the past in itself: the past, free from all the great Abstractions such as were now supposedly stalking the Meadows, peopled only by men such as himself and the machines they might fashion. A regular world, where one's sanity could always resort to certain fairly rigid standards whenever it was in danger of breaking; standing, as it were, on a good solid plain and not perched on the cliff's edge getting ready to jump.

But then Yarrow would come storming up, an hysterically laughing Tapp following in his wake, spouting damnation and Scripture, or else the crew would make itself known and the magic would be ended. Smythe would retreat back into his little, miserably defended stronghold of holy droppings and disavow any allegiance to Krysale Abbey or Iriam; all he wanted to do then was to go to the Meadows and Die like all those on the side of Right Ought to Do. Yarrow would pound him on the back, hurl some presumably encouraging chapter and verse at him; then Yarrow would always turn and toss some further bit of Scripture at the world. But all that VanRoark could see of the world was the Sea, shining with luminous fish and night creatures, ghost-osprey circling the ship and the stars. Then he was sick of Yarrow and the ship, but not with the terrified sickness he had caught from the insect on the Greenbelt. This was an immature, but still rather righteous sickness; by now VanRoark had begun to see his person becoming cluttered and filled up with vague, half-formed feelings and sensations, things that he had never even conceived of at his home city. Even now, less than three months away from Admiralty Square, he looked back upon himself in those days with the weary, bittersweet cynicism that is the fate of youth when it steps, or thinks it does, beyond its previous limits. A world was growing within him, one composed of bits and pieces of ocean, the fragmented histories of five hundred nations, prophets, dogma, time and dying men.

It was this last thing that prevented him from the nearly inevitable blunder of youth which, once having discovered the outlined world inside itself, wallows in it and mutters to itself, utterly convinced that its situation is unlike any other in all creation. They lose their humility in self-inflated bitterness, the young, and wear their self-inflicted scars like the wounds of real wars and sorrows. But the dying men, his association with their real sorrows and torments, those men who did not bother to examine and parade themselves, kept VanRoark's mind from dwelling too much upon itself and thus shutting out all else. It was hardly a love, nor was it any sort of awe, although both Tapp and Smythe inspired their own particular brands of admiration in VanRoark; it was more as if VanRoark, upon finding the gradually assembling fragments within himself, used this knowledge and feelings as a kind of lens through which he could glimpse, however briefly, the dreadfully complete worlds of the two men.

They were the ends of time, human wrecks crawling to their deaths, but leaving behind them a history, and in this perhaps even one or two works that might be worthy of being called just. It was only through men such as these, who had allowed themselves to sense the meaning of their agony, that the Wars could be fought; it was they who built and now would tear down.

In moments alone, VanRoark would muse upon Tapp and Smythe, considering them coldly and granting them ironic titles, which made them look even more pitiful and ridiculous than they were already: The Final Culmination of Human Evolution (when he saw Tapp reeling about the deck after dinner, his ulcer bleeding bright and clear in the setting sun), Protector of the Divine Plan of Creation (when he saw Smythe trying so very hard to explain Good and Right to their illiterate, malarial cabin boy). But then survivors are always more pitiable than the dead.

There was Yarrow, but he only had a walk-on in all this,

VanRoark sagely concluded. He touched nothing, allowed nothing he did not approve of to touch him, and scarcely cared for anything save the sound of his own voice. VanRoark imagined a ship similar to their own, but now sailing north to the Meadows, loaded with men he would eventually be trying to kill; doubtlessly, on board there was a Yarrow, distinguishable from their own only in the name of the Great Abstraction with which he defined his own faith.

Then, with a dispassion that is also usually alien to youth, discovering that one had lived and would soon die, he tried to fit himself into this and found he could not. At times he was the avenging angel going to serve his God and his Plan, but despite Timonias, he could never feel quite as majestic as the phrase demanded; neither was he of the race of men that had built world after world and then left when their time had properly arrived; not yet, at least. This was no good; now he was nothing, going to a probable death for no reason at all. The Sea perhaps? That would be his heritage and his ally, he decided.

He supposed that once there had been those who had built the great ships and sailed upon them, those of the wanderer caste. The Meadow Wars again receded in his mind and the voyage virtually supplanted it in his immediate thoughts. He began to take up with the crew, not for any companionship but only to learn their arts.

X

Against the ocean there was usually the coast, always on the starboard side, for few vessels cared to venture out of sight of land if they could help it. The lands south of Enador were quite desolate, high rock cliff faces usually screening inland areas from the Sea most of the time. Gradually, though, the land dipped down to sea level. They were getting into warmer latitudes, where warm currents from the southeast fed the mangrove and cypress forests of the great Enstrich Marshes before they swirled out to Sea again, to touch lush Kyandra and some of the lesser of the Dresau Islands. The gray and sand colors of the coastal territories gave way to a flat line of green that turned to a solid carpet when viewed from the maintop. They sailed past the Marshes for almost a week; by day, VanRoark would borrow the captain's glass and survey the steaming wall, watching the huge snakes and lizards that lived there moving through the trees of the water, their heads awash like rotting logs, and the gold and pink birds that rose at their passing. At night, if the moon was bright enough, he could see the eyes and crystal hides of the reptiles weaving through the breathing darkness.

Tapp became more sober as they bordered the Marshes. VanRoark at first thought that the appearance of some kind of untarnished fertility still left on the land had lifted his spirits. But it was only that they were approaching Cynibal. Tapp grew hopeful and despairing by turn, knowing that if he actually landed there he would probably be hanged for treason, Bournmouth III's Curia having a very long memory; still, it was a home that he had not seen for quite a few years.

The swampy coastline died out, to be replaced by level sand beaches that shaded off into rolling hills covered with pale bayonet grass. Joshua trees and cottonwood broke up the monotony.

Tapp began drinking again; in his memories, the grass had been green and fair, like the Greenbelt was supposed to have been once. There were ruins too, the occasional hull of a gutted tank, half overgrown in the murderous grass, lying beside cottonwood groves. Then came the cities, the small ports that grew larger as they neared the entrance to Blackwoods Bay, the harbors silted up like VanRoark's home, the streets deserted and the walls already beginning to show the impact of the wind.

VanRoark had heard stories of this nation from the pilgrims who had come to the cathedral, of its power and beauty, how almost alone it still held itself together and worked its old sciences and arts. Great ships were supposed to have called at Blackwoods Bay, where pumps still brought oil up from the Sea's bed, where the towers still trickled out fuels and lubricants; then the ships would go back to their home nations at the edge of the world.

VanRoark wanted to ask Tapp about all this, and what had happened, even though he obviously did not know either; but by the time they sailed into the Bay Tapp had returned to his usual stupor, trying to keep himself unconscious so that he would never see his dead Cynibal.

So Smythe, when he could get away from Yarrow's undiminished ravings and chokings, fearfully climbed the maintop to VanRoark and offered what small things he still remembered. The northern shore of the Bay had been Cynibal's, the southern one having belonged to Ihetah-Incalam, and it was like a miles'-long tangle of thorn bushes, wreckages of wells and refineries, oiling docks. Fires were burning amid the tangle and would keep burning, Smythe said, until the wells went dry, perhaps two hundred years from now.

VanRoark had lived with ruin long enough to be at home with these, but the immense scale of the fires made them something apart, as if they had just been destroyed and had yet to die utterly. The worst ones were the offshore wells, natural gas, according to Smythe; there the flame just burst from the Sea, as if giving birth to something vast and terrible, steam and boiling water ringing its pale blue and yellow base.

Where the fires lived on the land, in the iron shrubbery of fallen, cracking towers and distillation units, their constant heat had melted the steel so that the sharp outlines and angles softened and bowed down grotesquely near the flames.

Ships were there too, perhaps those of which the pilgrims had talked: tankers and merchant ships burned and blackened and melted by the fires, sunk at their docks with the dirty, oil-slicked water painting their sides in sickly rainbow diffractions.

Tapp would just sit on the bow, blind drunk and completely insensitive to the coast or to Yarrow's running commentary on the vanity that had called down such a fate on Cynibal. And then as Yarrow rose to some particularly emotional pitch, his lungs would reassert their presence and he would scuttle to the side, dribbling thin trails of blood and saliva down the side. The crew thought the passengers a most amusing collection of freaks and idiots.

They were bound for the western end of the Bay, to a port called Mount Soril, where they would provision for the uncertain journey south and then west. Predictably, Mount Soril was no less devastated than Cynibal; the city had been one of Ihetah-Incalam's most prosperous ports, but that nation had apparently suffered the same end as its northern sister. It had been the plague and its attendant madnesses at Mount Soril. It was still inhabited, now by maniacs and paranoiacs, people who worshiped the sun because they feared the night.

VanRoark went ashore with some of the crew in search of provisions and water; they were armed and really had little to fear. VanRoark found the place weirdly enchanting. There was very little physical destruction, aside from a complete lack of any maintenance for more than ten years, he estimated. The sight of Soril's poor citizens wandering through the overgrown gardens, the clogged pools and gently crumbling buildings awakened an odd pity in him.

They were utterly alone; the diseases and gases of someone's inspired national policy had robbed them of any recourse, not the mouthings of Yarrow, or Tapp's drink, or even the sorry self-delusions of Smythe. Time had ended for them; they were beyond the reach of anything.

Even the crew could sense this, although their feelings were never articulated past the stage of superstitious fear. They had stolen all they needed, their presence having hardly been acknowledgd by Soril's people. The few questions they had asked had been answered in a highly elliptical and confusing manner. There had been a war eight years ago between the two nations in which they had wiped out each other. Now the only difference was that Ihetah's dead were still walking around, whereas Cynibal's were comfortably underground. The former had used conventional explosives hoarded and purchased from traders like the *Garnet;* the latter nation had used gases and synthetic plagues that had been mined up from the seemingly inexhaustible Armories and brought overland at great cost.

Smythe had come ashore that last day, and he had questioned the comparatively clear-headed girl who had told VanRoark about the war. "Why did it begin?" Smythe asked gently.

"It was a good fight, sir, a very good fight, fought with honor and courage and cunning on both sides."

"I'm sure, but how did it begin?"

"You know, for a while there—before the war—it could be very fine, you know, the two of us; all very peaceful and lovely. But if it had to end, we guess the war was a good end for it. It was a good fight, sir."

"But who started it?"

"What?" she asked blankly.

"The war! Your well-fought war!" Smythe exploded and at once felt sorry for it.

"Oh yes." She tugged lightly at a curl of auburn hair; VanRoark began to feel sick with helplessness. She was beyond his touch no matter what he might do, no matter what he might say. "Well, I guess we, they . . . oh yes . . . yes!" Her eyes sparkled briefly and she looked up at the men for the first time; she was smiling. "The war began . . . something so little . . . I think someone wrote a book and old Bournmouth thought he was in it and . . ." Then she lost control and began to shake with close detonations of hysterical laughter. ". . . Book, Christ! a book . . ." She really thought it was funny, by the looks of her. VanRoark glanced at Smythe, wondering whether he should be embarrassed or wait for the end of the joke.

Slowly, the laughings and chucklings grated off into long, partially suppressed sobs and curses. She looked up at them once more, her hair matted and the dirt on her face streaked and stained by tears; then she closed her reddened eyes, which might have been opal or green or gold near the pupil but which were now only dull gray, and wandered away from them.

"Should we do anything . . . anything?" VanRoark asked Smythe, hoping that the old man might have remembered an appropriate cure for the disease from his Libraries.

"Yes, leave. Away from this place, Amon, now." He began walking quickly toward the piers, away from the girl; then he stopped and turned to the younger man. "And look at this place—look at her again, once; that's how all of it will be soon."

VanRoark was unprepared for this. "But the Meadows," he blurted.

"Not even that, I think. Not even our Meadows will stop it." Smythe's voice was harder than he had ever heard it before. That was the bad thing, that there was no confusion in it, as if he were speaking about ships or history, things that at the bottom of his heart, he knew.

XI

VanRoark was relieved to notice that once they had shipped out of Mount Soril and were heading clear of the Bay, Smythe returned to his normal, pathetically confused character; he was much more comfortable to live with that way.

They stayed close to the well charted northern shore as they had on the way in, where the fires by land and Sea guided them at night. Cape Lane was soon rounded and they glided down Ihetah-Incalam's gentle seacoast. The harsh, blasted tangles of Cynibal's cities were replaced by calm white sand beaches and buildings of soiled, crumbling stucco. The remnants of flags were still fluttering from some flagpoles along the seawalls and esplanades. Figures could be seen wandering along the beaches or through the dead towns; once in a while one of the figures would see them and burst into sudden action, yelling and beating his fellows on the back to attract their attention. Then he might run down to the Sea or out along a pier, raise his arms to call to them; but no call ever came. The figure would stand there a bit, arms open to the air, saluting. The arms would lower hesitantly and the retreating figure would shake with suppressed sobs.

They could tell they had left Incalam behind, when the

people came running from the cities with swords in their hands. The architecture and atmosphere of the ruins were strange and alien to all but Smythe, who would smile at things they could not guess at. Tapp worried long and loud that they might run out of liquor; Yarrow was only loud.

The land was sere and charred, the grasses poisoned, the trees stunted, with nothing but bones and corpse-nations to mark the passage of men. VanRoark got progressively sicker of the skeletal coastline, deserts and salt marshes alternating with sterile cliffs of basalt and granite. He withdrew from Smythe, leaving the man to his incomprehensible joy as he recognized some feature of a gutted building or hulk lying awash on a reef. Even Tapp was abandoned for the time, or rather they both got the same idea at once.

Tapp was having to conserve his drink now, no one having any idea how far the Meadows might be, and he was rather reserved, at times even brittle, during the day. VanRoark supposed he slept a lot, as he was seldom on deck.

VanRoark only continued his daily session with the boatswain, a burly man named Prager, whose leprous hands were still proficient in knot-tying and the usual business of sailing. He was going to the Meadows for one thing: "A good little pistol, like the one my dad had before it was lifted. Real nice. Automatic, know? Little pearl around the butt, nice heavy feel to it."

"Is that all?" VanRoark would ask; he did not like talking with Prager, in spite of the man's friendliness.

"Well, mate, see this?" He held up his right hand so VanRoark could see the splotches of dirty white along its back and running up the small finger. "Pretty soon that won't be there; gonna tie a nice knot, pull it tight, take my arm back and there's still gonna be one or two fingers where I was holding it. So all you need for a gun is two fingers to hold it and one to shoot it. Gimme that and I can still keep this lot up and running." He motioned toward a group of men lounging in the shade of the upturned jolly boat. "And when that's gone, sir, I'm gonna have Sawdust over there make up a little sort of wooden hand with my automatic bolted right into it. I saw once, in Enador I think, how this guy had a fake hand, like the one I'm talking about, and he had this cord running up it and around his back so when he moved a muscle somewhere, the hand'd move." Prager smiled, almost in anticipation. "So it won't matter if I lose both of 'em. Little wood, little cord, nice gun from the Meadows and I'll still be the only one who can keep the old *Garnet* afloat and headed in the right direction."

VanRoark was repelled at this image, for he instantly conceived of Prager in the last stages of his illness: a wooden man with open bones and slop bucket head, the whole affair being run through a cobweb tangle of strings operated by the stomach muscles and the genitalia which, if not the most intelligent parts of Prager, were almost certainly the most rugged. Then he found it funny and would spend some of his off hours imagining the sailor with rusty nails already at his elbows and knees, a trapdoor mouth, and eyes that opened and snapped shut like a ventriloquist's dummy.

The high Meadows, he thought, the sacred ground where mankind was to spill the last of its blood. . . . It was growing hot again as they moved farther south. The coastline and Sea were perpetually bounded by an insubstantial haze. The wind was slack and irregular; sometimes, when it died entirely and the Sea went dead and oily smooth, he began to view his quest as unvarnished idiocy, and Timonias as a highly accomplished nut and charlatan, nothing more. Tapp and Smythe gradually lost the quixotic charm and courage with which he had formally endowed them. Yarrow, at times, seemed to be the only honest man on board; at least he did not try to hide the fact that he was an idiot and therefore did not have to be ashamed that he should be so taken by such a preposterous myth.

At that instant, Tapp was just an old, beaten man, one who could find no other refuge than liquor from his own failures and those of his similarly flawed world. The grand language deteriorated each time it was used again; the archaic usages that had seemed so wonderfully gallant in the submarine pens were as affected and boring as Yarrow's. In addition to all of these things, Tapp was a traitor, and the age of the nation state had not so completely vanished as to make this less of a blasphemy to some men. The bleeding sore on the back of his neck became a more appropriate emblem.

And why was he truly going to the Meadows? That was a bit harder for VanRoark. Ideally, this new Tapp he had constructed should be running as fast as possible in the opposite direction. But perhaps he had already been in the other directions and found only the things that had driven him from Cynibal; now there might be no place left for him but the Meadows. He would be dead within two years, that was known beyond any doubt, and it could be, as the little man had pointed out himself in one of his heroic drunks, that his death might be a gallant one. This last possibility momentarily grasped VanRoark's consciousness and he concluded that if Tapp had such a fine time proclaiming how he would die, then perhaps VanRoark might also pass some time in so pleasant a manner; he tried it once, snitching a little of Tapp's closely guarded brew and some of the crew's swill.

Actually it wasn't much, but he was tired and inexperienced, so the liquor worked with satisfactory efficiency. He got violently ill, of course (the worst part about *that* was being physically unable to escape Yarrow and his predictable sermon on the evils of drink), but before that he had almost enjoyed it for a while. He grew very quiet and peaceful, and once again the Sea with all its swarming life enchanted him: starlight glistened on the metallic sides of flying fish and barracuda—deeper down in the clear water the shadow forms of manta-rays, colonies of luminous bacteria clinging along the edges of their wings and barbed tails, glowed milk and turquoise. All was as it should be there, all calm and naturally complete, living in accordance with whatever plan or agency had created it. Where, he wondered, could Tapp's raging energy, anger, and defiant cynicism come from in such a peaceful world?

Then the twisted, agonizing howling of the land would sigh across to him and he tried to tell whether it was a man or an animal, and who was feeding on whom. The coast was nothing more than a black outline, like the manta-rays, but devoid of their cool luminosity.

For five days they had sailed past a salt desert that ran

only a few feet above sea level, almost to the horizon, where it met a range of low, iron red cliffs. The concrete and rusted steel foundations of the ruins rising above the flats with jarring abruptness were there, as they were everywhere else; collections of flying boats were occasionally seen gathered together, usually about a mile or two inland, the metal panels and fabric torn from their ribs. They looked like dead sailfish or marlin washed up by some storm, and slowly being picked apart by the sea gulls and salt lizards.

VanRoark thought of Smythe then; firstly, because he had been the one to identify the aircraft and even guess that the faded, black and yellow roundels and tail blazons meant they had once served a nation called the Synod; secondly, he thought of him because Smythe was dead too, although not half so beautifully as the planes. He was like the people in Mount Soril, dead but still walking.

It had been the dead men, he remembered, that he had so sagely concluded would truly fight at the Meadows. Now Smythe and Tapp were dead and nothing more. They had not even enough courage to determine their own motivations for the physical formality of death. VanRoark's drunken stupor heaved itself about, vaguely aiming at an anger with men who had allowed the learning of Krysale Abbey to vanish, or betrayed their own homeland, trading them for the doubtful myth of the Meadows.

Unconsciously, his hand felt along the ship's side, looking for an unused belaying pin to use first on Smythe and then on Tapp; he felt around the back of the board searching for one, when he touched something at once sandy and sponge-like, like an old cigarette someone had dropped. He held it up to the starlight; that was when he got sick, for it was Prager's little finger. The land had produced yet another ingenious variation on the usual afflictions of mankind, and Prager's mutated leprosy had cut straight through the finger, rotting bone and nerve alike. Prager, good-humored and stupidly resigned as ever, had left the finger there on purpose; when he heard about it in the morning he waved the cauterized red and white stump in VanRoark's face and laughed himself silly over the youth's still rebellious stomach.

XII

VanRoark recovered from this episode, though now he pursued his education in sailing as best he could alone; ashamed at the sorry treatment he had given Smythe and Tapp, he retreated even further from the two, seldom thinking very deeply about them or their motives.

They had been at Sea for quite some time now and not even several mildly successful expeditions ashore into some ruined city or rare patch of healthy vegetation for food and water helped much in fending off scurvy and pellagra; not even the *Garnet's* crew were having a very good time of it and there was brooding talk drifting aft from the forecastle at night. They were in no danger, the captain assured them, for the crew, normally a gutless lot anyway, were now even more cowed by their reduced numbers and the captain's monopoly on water and limes, all of which were kept in his cabin and would be instantly emptied into the Sea should any mutiny begin.

Presently, though, they began rounding more headlands, and weaving through a patchwork of islands and archipelagos. The sun shifted, until it rose astern and then on to starboard, over the land. The wind had also shifted and now spilled off the burning cliffs.

Here the territories were utterly unnamed and not even Smythe had the slightest notion of what flags might have flown over the infrequent ruins, or in the service of what gods those hulks might have sailed. But Tapp knew—some of it, anyway. The little man began to come on deck more often, to pace nervously up and down, his eyes flickering between the land and sky.

Every so often he would see something he thought he remembered from eleven years ago, and would scratch furiously at his wound until it bled; and if he did remember he would run for Smythe or VanRoark and point to it and tell how he had passed this very spot so many years ago. But he never seemed quite as sure as he would have liked to have been. He continued to pick at his neck and then he would have to raise a bucket over the side and wash the pus and blood off his hand. By this time the ruins, the devastated factory or church had been left behind.

VanRoark really began to worry about Tapp for, besides his sudden nervousness, he had once again stopped drinking, before sunset anyway. The pain of his disease, which the liquor had previously hidden, now served to once again increase his agitation and brittleness. But unlike the other times, Tapp continued to abstain. VanRoark would ask him if he was looking for anything in particular, some landmark perhaps. Tapp would murmur something indistinct and then move off, away from the younger man.

He continued to drink fairly regularly at night, though, when the ship would heave to along the unfamiliar coast, its jagged outline sometimes spotted with strange luminosities. Then Tapp's voice would come flowing richly out of the darkness: not with the old, quixotic ravings, but a doggeral song, over and over again, with the same words.

"Set amid the thorn trees . . ." The words were slurred but still recognizable.

"... her towers soaring high,
her sullen flags defiant against the cobalt sky,
old Brampton Hall, deserted, wounded, left to die,
by allies who turned and fled at Evil's battle cry.

"Then the lads of Brampton Hall, their rifles
in their hands,
stood and fought the darken'd hordes that strode
upon their lands.
So here's a cheer for Brampton Hall! yet her
stone walls stand
to strive and hold the fall of night against the
fall of man!"

The memory of the revelations he'd had about Tapp during

his drunk began to fade in VanRoark; the man had become more nervous, admittedly, but it was not like the dread he had shown near Cynibal. It was anticipation, unconnected with any real fear or despair. It seemed once again that perhaps a man like Tapp could fight at the Meadows and fight well.

VanRoark eventually got around to asking Smythe about this Brampton Hall. The librarian ran his hand through his thin straw hair and said that the only thing he could recall was legend.

There had been a battle, he said, a great one which had finally annihilated a power named Salassar or something like that, the power which had resisted utter defeat for almost a millennium. In commemoration of this battle a memorial had been established. Understandably, for the war had been fought in very strange ways, the monument soon became a shrine, the object of a great many pilgrims. A town grew up around it, one in which a great soldier, Thomas St. Clair Brampton, eventually settled and founded a dynasty. The land was barren and hostile, but his descendants, living by the talents of their swords and minds, established a powerful nation. The name of their home, Brampton Hall, was given to the whole territory.

Now, from there it was very dubious, Smythe pointed out. Supposedly, at one of the false-Armageddons, Evil had actually routed the forces of mankind and broken out of the Meadows, raging about and threatening to engulf the entire world. It was stopped at Brampton Hall, whose families, ironically, had declined to go to the Meadows in their lordly contempt for the prophets and their attendant promises and plans. By this time, the armies had reformed and were able to drive Evil back to the Meadows, there to fight another agonizing draw. Brampton Hall itself was virtually wiped out in the holding action, her people for the most part dead or dying and the rest scattering in disgust as far away from the Meadows as possible.

VanRoark waited until Tapp was reasonably drunk and as close to his old moods as he had been for weeks, and then he told him of the librarian's tale. "Ah, true, the lot of it." Tapp sighed. "Except of course, it could do with a bit more to it, more substance, you know. I'm telling you this all straight down because I've seen the Hall. It's built on the mountains overlooking the Burn; I guess it was that battle they sang about that made it that way, so bad and all." Tapp took a thoughtful pull on his bottle, and said, more to himself than VanRoark, "Then I wonder what the old Meadows look like." He closed his eyes and took a much longer drink as he began to remember.

He resumed after the liquor had burned itself out in his throat, speaking very quickly so as not to allow himself too much time for thinking of the Meadows. "Oh, you'll love the Burn, Amon; at least you'll see a ruin with real character, real substance: great stone and steel walls, feet thick, and iron hammerbeams where the roof used to be, each one almost as thick as this tub here."

"We're going there? I thought the Meadows . . . ?" VanRoark trailed off weakly.

Tapp grinned and reached back to scratch his sore. "This Burn is where our army is gathering. Can't very well have us show up piecemeal, without any organization or anything. You weren't listening very well to your prophet when he told you that part."

"I guess not," VanRoark answered back, at ease again in Tapp's company. "But now it's my turn to wonder: I wonder where Evil is gathering."

"And then you weren't listening to that part either."

The grin faded a bit from VanRoark. "Which part?"

"The part where he, whoever he was, called Evil. We could hardly have the Meadows without an Opposition, you know."

VanRoark was getting confused; he had not thought very much about Timonias lately and all that he could dredge up was a vague collection of impressions, even more incomplete and fragmentary than when he had first begun to forget, across from the Isle of Oromund. "He *also* called Evil to the Meadows, the same person?"

"Right." Tapp was not in the least upset by this, which only served to further VanRoark's distress. "Look, you must remember your Timonias calling to those other types too." Indistinct shapes, terrifying in their very lack of definition turned and heaved just below VanRoark's comprehension.

"I don't know; I don't remember."

"When I heard my man—Lord, I can't even remember his name! Old, decrepit sort, I think—eleven years ago, I'm almost positive that he appealed to both sides. I can't see how he could have helped but do that because, remember, the thing he told you about was History and how it had to end. Well, the Opposition is as much a part of that ending as we are, so doesn't it seem right that he should just state the facts and let each man take his pick? That is the whole idea behind the thing, you know."

"All right, maybe Timonias did say something to them. I don't know, but if he did, then it must mean that he could have been the chosen of Evil as well as Good. The distinction of what *he* was would have lain in *our* hearts and not his." Why, VanRoark asked himself, did Tapp seem to be getting more relaxed and natural as the progress of the argument led to some conclusions that had him approaching a near-panic?

Tapp calmly nodded that, yes, that seemed right.

"Then maybe, if Timonias was talking to us all—both them and us, I mean—he would have used the same words." VanRoark was talking very slowly now; how strange that he had never asked himself this: "Then it could mean that *we* are Evil, going to its army! Tapp, what if that's true?"

Tapp shrugged and took another drink.

VanRoark was now desperately trying to find ways out of the corner he had argued himself into. "You were there before, Tapp; how did it seem?"

"Seemed good enough for my tastes."

"But you're not sure, you could have been wrong . . . ?" VanRoark had almost said, *You could be betraying me.*

"Amon." Tapp raised his hand to VanRoark's shoulder to calm him, but changed his mind and only touched him lightly. "When I went to the Meadows for the first time it was with the full intention, as far as I could tell, of fighting on the side of Good; that's all. I heard the words, as much as anyone could hear such words, and I left to pledge my soul on the side of Light and God; if the same words are used for the Good as well as the Evil, then it's up to every man to sort out their real meaning, for himself, in his own heart and mind. The army you go to, the men you will die beside, they will be of the same substance as yourself; and if it turns out that you have come to the army of Night, it will be simply because that is what you are and to change that would be impossible. Like I said, though, I believe we are joining the right side."

"But you're still not absolutely sure," VanRoark fairly croaked. "Why are you going back if you're still not sure what you might die in the name of?"

Tapp smiled drunkenly at him. "I will die in the name of what I am, nothing else." He looked at VanRoark for a moment, as if trying to decide whether or not he should keep on speaking. "And what I am now, I think, is neither Good nor Evil. I think, I hope it's Brampton Hall; if I die in the name of that, then this trip and the years spent before it will have been right."

VanRoark waited, expecting some explanation of this remark; when none came and Tapp began drinking again and softly humming his song, the younger man gave a short cry that might have been rage, and ran forward, away from him.

XIII

Now it was VanRoark who spent most of his time below, in his hammock, going topside only during the night or early hours of the morning. He had absorbed so much, found so much that was confusing and frightening in people, been surrounded by the reality of the Great Abstractions brought jarringly to earth, devoid of any certainty as to their true identity. The ordered systems he had constantly tried to construct, first around the Sea and then around the infinitely elusive natures of Smythe and Tapp, were now reeling and crashing down upon each other and on top of the new, hideous uncertainties that Tapp had planted in his mind. His consciousness had been stretched from the empty sterility of the Greenbelt to the larger, more nebulous agony that was the entire world; this consciousness had acquired ruins, haunted ones. Questions he should have asked about himself years ago, or forgotten forever, came flooding in on the wake of his distress.

But strangely, the falling, colliding fragments eventually brought him a numbed peace. As they sailed northward he felt washed out; not clean, but nearer to the ordered, hollow confusion of death, the cleanliness of the shroud. He honestly wondered if he should ever feel anything again, ever experience another emotion to the bottom of his soul.

XIV

As a child, VanRoark had often sat on the breakwater of his home city and watched the tanners' hawks hunting the more sluggish terns and sea gulls which, in turn, hunted the fish that lived near the wreck-littered entrance. They were fairly large birds, molted white on the belly and underside of the wings, and a leathery tan on top. Exceedingly graceful, they would ride the winds for hours at a time, only moving their wings to gain an occasional few feet of height. When one had picked out a target, it would drift above it, all very easily and relaxed, and lift one wing in a languid roll; when the hawk was on its back, with its body pointed down about fifty degrees, the wings would suddenly be snapped in tight and it would fall. The easy, near-sleeping grace would become blurred with speed and violence; the talons would strike just behind the gull's neck, the power sometimes ripping the whole skull from the body.

The day was something like that, he thought later; they had been moving back into temperate latitudes and the old *Garnet* was behaving herself uncommonly well. He had been on deck, absently talking with Smythe, congratulating their good fortune at the progress of Yarrow's illness, for it meant he could only rarely indulge in his impassioned speeches.

It was after the noon meal (weevily hardtack and salt pork which had the prettiest little beetles living in it; the crew saved them and occasionally ran races). The lookout on the mainmast called down that there was a curious dot on the southern horizon. Then a pause; the dot was above the horizon and seemed to be slowly growing. All eyes swung aft, but everyone's bodies—except for Tapp and Smythe, who sprang for the ratlines and began to climb—were frozen.

VanRoark caught sight of the object, perhaps ten miles astern; then it was a hundred feet aft, abeam, and then forward, diminishing again.

It had been an aircraft, with longer and more graceful lines than the tanners'. VanRoark shut his eyes as soon as it had gone and examined the instant: not more than seventy feet off the water, triangular wings that were bent upward at their tips, a single sharkfin at the tail, dull black on the belly, wandering bands of olive and sand topsides. There were gaping holes in her near the wing roots that rounded into exhausts aft; and when she had been directly abeam of where VanRoark stood, the majestic silence of the craft's passage had been shattered by a rolling thunder that beat against his body, shook the *Garnet's* sails, and almost knocked Tapp and Smythe into the Sea.

Tapp was yelling hysterically from his perch: "Did you see that? Did you see her? Christ! Did you see her?" Then his tongue got wrapped up in itself as it tried to get out years of anticipation in five seconds.

Smythe was pleasantly dumbfounded in his thoughtful climb down to the deck. He said nothing then, but at dinner, when he could fit in a word between Tapp's endless and amazingly sober ravings, he said that it had been a bomber, a shade under two hundred feet long, capable of exceeding the speed of sound (VanRoark did not entirely understand that), and the last of her kind were supposed to have crashed and burned five centuries ago. He had had only a glance at her colors, but he could identify parts of at least three different national standards. There were two more he could not place. Smythe stayed up very late that night, something he had never done. Prager later told VanRoark that near dawn Yarrow had come up to the librarian, apparently unable to contain his decaying throat any longer on the subject of the plane. Smythe had beaten the living hell out of him.

VanRaork could feel a quickening, a compression of time about him that did not leave enough room to speculate on the Great Abstractions. He managed to look upon the uncertainties as things that fate had already decided for him. The Wars were still going on, he was sure of that now, and he was going to them. They were near now too, within human reach. The simply human took precedence and he wondered if, when men were trying to kill him, he would be able to stand and, presumably, try to do the same to them. Glory began to infect his mind.

The captain, who listened quietly and calmly with his ferret eyes and quick, nervous gestures to Tapp's uncontainable enthusiasm, was also moved. On the one hand he was rather disappointed to see such a powerful machine going to the Burn and the Meadows (even Tapp naturally assumed that the plane was going to join the same side as they), for it meant that removal of "cargo" from its present owners would be that much more difficult. Ruins were so much easier, no self-appointed patriots or saviors clinging to things which were almost useless to them but could turn a fair profit in the hands of an intelligent man.

However, the fact of the plane's being in operational condition had inflamed the captain's limited imagination. When Tapp had gone spinning off into the darkness and Smythe had followed behind, he dreamily explained to VanRoark the marvelous possibilities this situation presented to the circumspect businessman. If things as large as that aircraft were to be found gathering at the Burn, then why not steel ships powered by steam or even more marvelous things? There were twenty nations gunning for Enador and her monitors and steam frigate, and the man who delivered the proper ship could name his price.

As the evening wore on—VanRoark stayed even though he was both repelled and bored—the idea of piracy predictably arose. VanRoark could see the schemes and plans wiping aside the profit and loss sheets that had recorded the captain's dreary trade in rusting guns and stale explosives: a great battleship, her skeleton crew of fanatics sleeping the night; boats putting out from the *Garnet*, muffled oars, knives and metal wire around the crew's throats; then a new command for the captain, with all the world at his feet.

VanRoark left him to retire; naturally, he was unable to sleep and would have gone on deck, but he figured the deck belonged to Tapp and Smythe that night. Instead, he spent the night dreaming, half-awake, his ears still ringing from the aircraft's howling and the patchwork of insignia disrupting the smooth flow of her camouflage, the sun white on her glass, her exhausts yellow-red.

Once, just as he was dozing off, he heard a thumping and thought the sails were being shaken by the passage of another ship; he asked Prager about it in the morning and was told that it was probably only Yarrow hitting the deck.

XV

Five days after the camouflaged bomber had flown past them, Tapp spotted five glittering beads hanging below the sun, white chalk marks trailing behind them to the horizon. They looked at them now with less fear, and the crew hardly cringed when the dim, rolling report of their engines drifted down through the clear air. The captain brought his glass to bear on the formation, but it was so high above them that even he could see nothing more than a blinding metallic radiance.

The planes were over them for half an hour before they were lost from sight and their trails gently dispersed. Once again, VanRoark felt time shrinking and compressing; even the languid, peaceful passage of the formation reduced tomorrow to the next minute and the end of the world to tomorrow.

The first ship passed them the day after the formation;

Tapp was by now beside himself with anticipation, checking and endlessly rechecking his memories of the nations that had made up his army with the now prouder recollections of Smythe. *Lord,* VanRoark thought as she passed less than a quarter of a mile to port, *how lovely she is! How old and proud!* All battle gray in black trim, two twin turrets fore and aft, two stacks, a high bridge like a castle's keep, and a clipper bow plowing up the cyanogen water and turning it white; the pendent numbers 2470 were painted on her bridge and transom. The captain read out her name, *W. Lane. So curious,* Van Roark thought again, *that so beautiful a ship* ("Lord, 'Roark, look at 'er, must be turning thirty knots!") *should carry so dull a name,* especially when the wrecks of his world bore names like *Amethyst* and *Jewel* as they careened about the Sea.

Smythe hypnotically recited his usual list of particulars, armament figures, speeds, the nations she might have sailed for and how the ships of her type had acquitted themselves in storms and battles past. VanRoark saw only the fine, long sweepings of her lines and how cleanly she moved through the water, and the silken pennants that trailed for a hundred feet or more behind her masts.

Then she was gone. The *W. Lane* had given no acknowledgment of the *Garnet's* presence, had not even dipped a flag or displayed a signal lamp. But this bothered no one. Smythe, Tapp, and VanRoark were satisfied with her physical presence and to be reassured, again, that such things still existed. The captain and crew of the *Garnet* were relieved that the destroyer, so Smythe had termed her, had taken no notice of them; they welcomed the anonymity, for it meant that capturing her or one like her would be that much easier. The captain wondered how it would feel to have a steel deck under him and not have to worry which way the corrupted winds might be blowing at the moment. "*W. Lane,*" he rolled the name over in his mouth. Really, he would have to change that straight off. Only Yarrow was in any way irritated. He called it a sin for men to so treat their own creations that they handed ownership of their souls over to them.

VanRoark was rather disappointed when nothing was spotted the next day, nor on the one after that. He wondered if they had not, through some fantastic coincidence, stumbled into an area where the aircraft and ships just happened to be in their endless wandering, or if they had blundered onto one of the Sea's old graveyards, rife with ghosts and flying Dutchmen.

The coast was smooth and regular now, with the cooler water canceling the possibility of coral reefs. The scarcity of rivers or turbulences made sand bars a rarity too. They sailed at night, when the star or moonlight allowed. It was about midnight when Tapp's yelling, a little hoarse from all his fulminations, began shaking the *Garnet*. Men tumbled out of their hammocks and grabbed cutlass and ax, thinking they were under attack.

VanRoark ran on deck to find Tapp halfway up the foremast ratlines, pointing wildly at a rising headland to the northeast. "What is it?" he called up.

"Look, 'Roark, over there, on top of that rise. See it? See it?" Tapp waved in the direction of the coast.

VanRoark squinted but could see nothing. He tried again, this time moving back and forth slightly, to silhouette anything against the stars. He began to make out some skeletal structures, bare beams and irregular walls separating themselves from the larger darkness of the headland. "I see it now. What is it?"

"Brampton Hall, 'Roark!" Tapp fairly screamed.

"You said it overlooked the Burn, where the army'd be." VanRoark was vaguely aware of the delighted hysteria that was creeping into his voice too.

"On the north side of it. Soon as we round those cliffs we'll see them." A pause while Tapp's eyes swept the ruins again. "Brampton Hall!" he exploded.

Smythe came on deck, tucking his shirt into his trousers and wiping the sleep from his eyes. VanRoark pointed out the outline of the building. "Goddamn," he muttered thoughtfully.

Most of the crew was up, leaping about the deck or through the rigging, absently rigging flags of truce and weapons, not one of them really having any idea of what they should do. Yarrow, for once, was dead quiet.

VanRoark recalled the trite novels of his boyhood, what few there had been, and thought that now it would get very quiet, like the flowing peace of the tanners' hawks before they hit. But the night was underlaid with small, distant hummings and roars. As they moved northward, rounding the headlands, the noises grew more emphatic, first absorbing the gentle slap of the Sea, against the *Garnet*'s hull, and then intruding upon normal conversation. Vivid, sharp eruptions of sound began to break up the monotone, lacing it through with violence and power.

The headlands where Brampton Hall itself rested rose against the welkin to become a rather sizable line of near-mountains curving away and rounding up into the north, where they dissolved into the horizon. Cradled between these hills and the Sea was the army. Even Tapp was struck silent. It looked as if the *Garnet* were sailing directly into a star cluster, whose brilliance shimmered out to them across the surface of the calm Sea. Lights, more than VanRoark had ever seen, tapestried the dark earth with everything from the cold, unwavering shine of electrical bulbs to the rainbow shades of altars and votary lamps. Shapes and colors, nothing more than moving specks of blackness at this distance, hovered around the lights, occasionally separating themselves as fire shone through silk or upon burnished armor and was then reabsorbed.

A sudden call from the lookout shattered the spell. In their fascination with the glittering Burn, almost no one had noticed that the bay to which they were now sailing was filled with sailing boats and steamships. As they lowered the main and foresails, proceeding only on staysail and jibes, they saw fire-reflected shapes on the water as well as on land. The standard navigation lights of white, orange, and pale blue swept out from the coast to meet them on the hulls of five hundred sailing ships. Most looked to be as miserable as the *Garnet*, but others lay tall and proud, their gilt work fresh-painted, their hulls slick in the water, their brass cannon clean and warm in the lights.

VanRoark caught a low whistle from the captain and an order to edge the *Garnet* over to port. VanRoark looked to his left and saw gray walls rising from the Sea, walls with anchor chains stuck into them and pendent numbers of white and gold. Their superstructures were dull in the army's light and they towered above the *Garnet,* sharply outlining themselves against the stars. VanRoark thought he spotted the *W. Lane* and was amazed at how much larger were the others moored near her. Specter shapes in white and light tan moved upon the warship's decks: turrets, forest-masts with strange wire tangles wound about them, and flags stirring tiredly in the light air; fine lines and ancient metals passed by him as they moved toward the beach.

The captain recovered his senses after a while and, much as he might have liked to pick out his future command then and there, deemed it wiser to anchor and await daylight before he made any concrete plans. The hook was let down about a half mile offshore, between a four masted schooner from the Isle of Oromund and a destroyer like the *W. Lane,* which still chose to carry the standard of the long-broken North Cape Confederation.

Tapp decided to get drunk and spent most of the night on the quarterdeck, sitting on the wheelhouse, singing "Brampton Hall" and other old songs until he passed out. The crew would have shut him up but when any of them advanced upon him, he would only swing out his saber and sing all the louder. His fingers were wet with liquor and his own blood.

VanRoark and Smythe climbed to the maintop and for hours silently looked about them and through the universe they had entered, the ships and the roarings. They saw, past the gray ships to port, a single, unbroken line of stone that might have been the facing for some quay or causeway of undetermined length. More lights moved up and down this wall, some descending from the night and slowing to a stop, others rolling along it with increasing speed until they bulleted free and screamed off, their flight marked by the deep whistling of Smythe's first sighted lone bomber—and then by the far burble of the second formation.

Around three, when the false dawn was beginning to take hold behind the encircling hills, a fog crept in from the Sea, shrouding and softening the lights, blurring and confusing distances, wrapping the *Garnet* up inside the army's universe. Shapes and shadows of ships and aircraft, their activity now much diminished and the lights reduced in number, moved toward them with liquid delicacy and then receded, dancing about the old *Garnet* and her plotting crew. VanRoark guessed they still had more than an hour to go before dawn, which the mist would obscure for another hour anyway, and decided to turn in along with Smythe. Tapp had been unconscious for quite a while and was peacefully sprawled on the deck, his sword in one hand and an empty liquor tin in the other.

No one saw Yarrow during the night and he was not on board the next morning. The captain figured that the fanatic must have slipped overboard in the fog and made it ashore before any of them were up. Tapp did not entirely discount the possibility that the crew had murdered him for the jeweled holy books he had once said he was carrying with him. VanRoark surprised himself at how little emotion he felt at this thought—and even at the humor—for at least the poor old fool would have died where he wanted to, the absence of an Heroic Struggle Against Evil being but a minor omission in Yarrow's pilgrimage. But then, thought VanRoark, progressively more amused with this line of conjecture, perhaps he had put up a brave fight, and if the captain and crew of the *Garnet* were not as evil as Salassar was supposed to have been, they were not, by the same token, possessed of snow-white souls; and if they were then, in some measure, sworn to the flag of Night, it would mean they had defeated the adherent of Light. So it appeared that yet another Armageddon, one smaller than most, had been bungled. At least Yarrow, whether he was among his fellow believers on this world or the next, was happy.

XVI

VanRoark thought that what he had seen the previous night would have insulated him in some way against what he might see in the light of day. While he was lying in his hammock and later getting dressed, he tried to prepare himself to be disappointed by the reality of the army. In a way he was, for the steel ships numbered only nine and not a thousand, and parked atop the stone wall, now revealed as a causeway that stretched from the beach to the horizon, were not more than twenty-five aircraft of varying sizes.

But in themselves, each of them represented more power than any great nation his home world might be able to muster. As he forgot their numbers and concentrated upon individual examination, VanRoark became aware of just how much the night and then the fog had distorted distances and proportions. The *W. Lane,* the smallest of the nine, now appeared even greater in the crowded anchorage while the largest, a battleship of incalculable destructive power, loomed over the sailing ships clustered near her, and cast her morning shadow far out to Sea.

They were towed ashore in the *Garnet's* longboat along with one or two members of the crew who had honestly decided to throw their lot in with the army. The captain was still on board, briefing his chosen spies for their preliminary tasks.

Close inshore, they passed by the armed merchant cruiser that had brought Timonias to VanRoark's city. The rust was still scabbed about her plating and the gun tubs still marred the graceful lines. There were four other converted merchant ships moored around Timonias' ship, all in varying states of disrepair. The largest was also in the best shape, a tanker only a little smaller than the battleship farther out in the anchorage. The gloss black hull contrasted sharply with her spotless white topsides. As they rowed past her, VanRoark could see that her broad decks had been cleared of pumps and transfer pipes; a twin line of big field guns began aft of the forecastle, broke around the forward superstructure and then continued aft, their barrels and recoil mechanisms shining with preservative grease.

There was almost no surf and they landed easily. The crew stared at what lay before them and then pushed hurriedly back to the Sea and the *Garnet*. Before VanRoark, Smythe, Tapp and the two who had deserted the *Garnet* sprawled the army: colors, colors swirling and dancing at every hand. Armored men mounted on horses with silken covers galloped back and forth before them, maces and lances held in their gleaming hands, silk pennons trailing from their crested helmets.

Tents fanned out in a random manner from the beach, redoubling the riot of colors with their gay patterns and designs; before many stood a staff or an ensign of some great family or nation or noble order. VanRoark could pick out at least twenty identifiable standards from where he stood, and Smythe said that of those he could place, at least half were of nations he had thought dead or scattered past recalling: the dolphin and seabird crests of the Dresau Islands naval aristocracy; the star constellations of the lands of the House of Raud; the mailed fist and pegasus of Mourne, ringed with a circlet of black oak leaves in penance for some ancient, forgotten wrong; the horse mane and sun disk devices of Larine's barbarian nobility; enameled, chain mail banners from the mountain kingdoms of Iannarrow, Enom, Howth; lion, unicorn, and hippogriff painted shields before the tents of men from Mountjoy and Kirkland and Kroonstadt; the anchor and osprey flag of Enador could be seen flying among a thousand others. VanRoark turned back to the harbor and picked out the low riding form of one of the city's river monitors. *Goddamn! Even the capitalists are here*, he thought. And for every one he could identify there were a hundred that were beyond even the librarian's knowledge.

They walked slowly up from the beach, swimming through the colors and press of bodies, for the types of men easily outnumbered the crests and colors they had first seen. It was like a city fair, when such things were still being held; never in all the world, not even in Enador's brawling markets and wharves, had he sensed such activity and apparent purpose. Here, a thing was being *done,* men were at work on things and not sitting on their fat asses waiting for something to walk up and club them to death.

Lord! The air itself was as alive and electric as the torrent of colors and people. VanRoark felt his head lighten and his joints partially dissolve as they walked, first down one avenue lined with stalls peddling newly-caught fish and lobster, then down another where large, especially gaily colored tents had rather tough looking women standing beside them, even at this hour of the morning. Tapp considered the tents closely, grunting approval when he caught the eye of someone he liked—and then groaning at his lack of money. VanRoark supposed that even the Army of Justice and Light was still made up of normal men who had to live while they were waiting. Smythe had already disappeared into one of the tents.

They walked south along the seaward edge of the camp, pavilion after bright pavilion passing to their left, great, heavily carved sailing ships riding at anchor on their right or careened up on the beach having their bottoms scraped. Gradually, the camp sites thinned out as they climbed up into the mountains toward Brampton Hall's ruin. It was about noon and they were almost to the summit of the headlands when they stopped for a lunch of black bread and cheese that VanRoark had purchased on one of the market avenues. Prices were much steeper than they had expected. After hassling at several shops and idly pricing items they could never afford no matter what their normal price—things like pistols or chain mail shirts—VanRoark correctly guessed that Enador had sent one of her precious river monitors to guard her merchants, not to die in the name of God or Creation. When they talked to Smythe later in the week, he confirmed that Enador's commercial ventures, along with some of the other trading nations and cities present, went further than selling inanimate goods. That was why most of the shops and brothel tents were near the shore, for they could be more easily protected by the guns of their guardian ships.

These ideas depressed VanRoark more than he thought they should have. After all, was he not a jaded traveler, a wanderer who had left all this world had to offer him to go and seek his just end? But the organization, the emotionless calculation of it all really upset him for a time. Tapp, on the other hand, was fairly philosophical about the whole thing, arguing that if a fellow wanted to make some honest gold out of the end of the world, then who was to say he was wrong? None of this did much to counter VanRoark's recurring doubt that he had come to the right army.

But now they turned on the mountain's slope and, panting from the climb, stared at the carpet the army spread before them. The flat blurring colors and planes they had seen from sea level were now tilted upward, swirling, turning, colliding like buckets of dye suddenly dumped into a whirlpool. As they looked down to the north and northeast, they could see the nondescript, bland horde of tents and shelters in which men like themselves were forced to exist because of their inability or refusal to submit to Enador & Co.'s gougings.

As the density of the camps grew, so did the colors. First a single stripe of red or orange silk, or perhaps a small family banner sewn to a canvas wall, an hereditary suit of mail, ancient and oiled, gleaming by a doorway. Then came the close packed heart of the army, its random, directionless avenues with their chromatic floods and harsh flashing metal; men mounted on strange beasts, gryfons and other winged creatures that flew above the bazaars and among the myriad flags. There was life compressed, even as time had become compressed for VanRoark, consuming and rioting with itself as if it had to satiate its last desires, before leaving for the Meadows.

There were no priests dressed as the two thought priests should, black and somber as befitted their mission in all this. Nor was there anything which might be taken for a church or temple. Tapp, however, said he had spotted several private shrines inside various tents.

The colors began to dull and fade out as the army once again began to thin out to the north; but instead of simply dying out, the tents and encampments ended abruptly; there was a stretch of several hundred feet and across that VanRoark could dimly make out the priestly dignity of canvas-shrouded field artillery and armored vehicles. They stood at the foot of the mountains, which curved east, and then straight north in a huge semicircle; the northern edge, instead of looping back and closing with the Sea, was split by a river gorge and then appeared to die away into grasslands. More formidable ranges, olive and dark gray, defined the horizon far past the grass plain.

Drawn up between the river and its delta were the tanks and colorless tents of what the main body of the army called the rim nations, for they lived at the edge of the world and, presumably, at the edge of chaos. Tapp said they were the lads of Brampton Hall, and they were not going to the Meadow Wars—they had merely come home. Then he laughed and VanRoark wondered if it was a joke.

At the eastern edge of the army, where the mountains dipped to allow the river to pass, there were four or five long, olive and tan camouflaged vehicles; they were articulated and made up of many separate cars. Tapp called them land trains and said that the longest of them stretched for more than a thousand feet. Moving westward along the border of the army were massed the artillery of the rim nations and their armored trucks and tanks; even at this great distance from them, hulking, brutal forms were clearly visible, even the red and purple flags flying from their masts and aerials. Small figures in tan and black walked in front of them or crawled over their vast exteriors.

The ranks of guns and vehicles were broken at irregular intervals by command tents and temporary buildings, again spined with radio masts and disk antennas. So strange, VanRoark thought as he looked at them, distance dissolving as it had in the fog last night; they were so quiet and firm beside the main body of the army and its erupting life. Soft, rippling colors blazoned on flags of a hundred different nations, and heritages lived below him, even though they awaited the signal to end Creation. Then north, across the hard crystalline soil that gave the Burn its name, the rim nations, almost sleeping, were strangely touched with the sadness of ruins; it was so quiet over there, no sounds drifting up to them over the blare of the army's shops and whorehouses.

The guns and tents, in loose order like tombstones, ambled westward until they reached a point about a third of a mile from the beach. There the aircraft of the rim nations (he was already beginning to identify them as something apart from the army) waited, one or two moving out of line, briefly catching the sun on their polished hulls and wings; they taxied out onto the horizon-reaching causeway. Tapp said it had been built by Brampton Hall, though for what reason he could not guess.

There was a bridge-like structure piercing the causeway two hundred yards from the beach, most probably to let the ships north to the Meadows. They rolled out over this, and then gained speed as their wing roots or tails burned pale yellow. Finally, the rim nations sent some noise up into the hills.

VanRoark followed the pathetically few aircraft as they tumbled westward and then lifted free, gaining sudden grace once they were rid of the earth. Their sound smothered the sea-roaring of the army and for a moment there was only the ground which he stood upon and the shining, silver bobbins streaming across the sky for some unknown purpose.

The ships he had seen last night and that morning, the five gray warships and three merchant cruisers, the tanker with its decks crammed with artillery, were moored nearest the causeway; flags dipped from ancient masts as the craft took off from the causeway, and the infrequent flashings of signal lights winked under their shadowed superstructures.

VanRoark thought at first that the ships and the encampments of the rim nations were already dead; but the planes and signal lamps showed that that was not yet true. They were only tired, sick with age, and traveling toward a resting place that seemed to be forever receding from them; thus the sadness. They had been running so very long.

A week after they had climbed up the mountain to Brampton Hall, he had chanced to wander across the dividing strip between the main force of the army and the rim nations. There had been very few persons around, at least compared to the eternal bustling of the army. He had walked up and down the rows of tanks and big guns, and when he counted them there did not seem to be so many.

There had been a man leaning up against the tires of a howitzer's split trail carriage, the watchworks of its sighting mechanism disassembled on a white sheet in front of him. He was naked to the waist, lean and deeply tanned, but that could have been his natural body color; either way, the contrast to his blue eyes was most striking. There was a tattoo of an armored Death, mounted on a pegasus, on his left forearm, and under it the words, *656th Airborne—the Devil's Own.*

They talked of inconsequentialities for a while, the price of women and swordfish steak, the lack of any life on board Timonias' old cruiser.

VanRoark mentioned the man's tattoo and asked where his planes were.

"Crashed on the way here. Probably still there in the, uh, North Cape Confederation's old lands; it's cold up there. We didn't think we were going to make it down in one piece, 'cause see, we got into these fjords. Walker set us down all right, though. We lost him a while back in the Barrens." His voice was slow, he was paying much more attention to rebuilding the sight than talking.

"How long ago was that?"

"Around ten, eleven years," he answered absently.

VanRoark was taken back a bit by this; he may have heard the call for the same Armageddon that Tapp had. "And you've been traveling since then to get here?"

"Around that, a little less, though, 'cause we got here about four months ago. And even then, we didn't spend that much time moving. The worst part was fishing all we could out of the water and then finding enough fuel for our tractors. We even rigged one up with a steam engine." He laughed a little at that.

VanRoark waited but apparently the man had nothing more to say on that particular subject; he kept working on the sight, carefully recoiling a small spring back into its gauge casing. "Don't you have anything else besides guns?" VanRoark mumbled more to himself than to the man as he glanced down the ranked barrels of howitzers and long rifles, steel cables rigged from breech castings to muzzle brakes to correct temperature warping of the bores.

The man heard this, or part of it, and for the first time put down his gears and miniature screwdrivers. "What?" he said, looking at VanRoark.

The younger man was immediately conscious of a slip in courtesy. "Well, I meant that the rest of the army has its weapons, of course, but they've also got other things; they've got their women and their musicians and entertainers. I think some men even brought their whole families, kids and all. And their shops and stalls, like a whole city was just dropped right down here and was setting up to stay forever."

"They could do that," the man said sourly. "We don't have these things. I know that. All we got are guns, and you know why?"

VanRoark shook his head, no, he did not.

"Because that's all they left us, dumb-ass!" he hissed unexpectedly, jabbing a finger in the direction of the army. "All those bleeding bastards left was the guns we could hold. Everything else, every good or beautiful thing we ever tried to set up in this world, they managed to queer or tear down.

"You know where I come from?" He did not wait for an answer. "How the hell could you, it doesn't even have a name any more! All you'd have to know is that it was dying and with all our power we couldn't do a thing about it. Every time we poked our hands outside of our lands because we needed some oil or some ore or even some clean water, they jumped us, from the front if they had the guts, but usually from the back. Sneaking in at night and slashing some dude's parachute and then repacking it all nice and careful, or putting some sort of bomb into one of our ships."

The man sank back against the cracked tires and wiped the sweat from his bald, bronzed skull. "Okay, man, you've heard my genealogy; get back to your army before you really ruin my afternoon."

VanRoark got up and began walking away, but could not resist asking a question: "Why are you here?"

"To die." The other shrugged, bending back over his work. "This is the army of Right and Good and all. That's what your prophet said, didn't he?"

"I don't remember what the old bastard may have said. I'm here just because I'm sick and tired of all this, that's all."

"Not for Brampton Hall?"

"Never heard of it."

But that was a week after he had seen Brampton Hall for himself and had already begun to guess that this was what would be told him should he ever venture into the rim nations' camp.

They had reached the ruins of Brampton Hall by one in the afternoon, the army having smeared itself into a mass of indistinct rippling movements, edged by the slag-covered mountains and the camouflaged rim nations. In front of them soared the walls and blasted towers of the Hall, remnants of chain mail banners still flying from warped iron flagpoles. It was as huge as Tapp had said and for the first time in all his travelings, except when he had sat alone in the maintop with nothing but the Sea and a shadow ship below him, had he felt such peace. This was doubly strange, for the Hall, a term which included a whole complex of buildings and walls along the spine of the mountains, had obviously been the scene of a great struggle. Bullet holes, nearly eroded smooth but still recognizable, were splattered all over the walls; iron roofing beams of incredible size twisted down from their mountings as if some fantastic heat, like that of Blackwoods Bay, had made them bow before it.

VanRoark walked with Tapp into the main compound, almost a quarter of a mile square. Grass was growing there; not anything green or vaguely suggesting complete health but, still, an enormous change from the scorched sterility of the Burn and the slagged-down mountains. Mosses reached up the chipped and shattered walls along with a stunted form of ivy, trying to heal their wounds.

There were even bits of stained glass remaining in the arched windows of the Hall itself, fragments suggesting family crests or the lives of great men. VanRoark marveled at this especially, until he saw that the glass was almost seven inches thick.

Although there were traces of the ancient battle in the Hall—someone's femur bone was crushed into calcium dust just under the tarn and VanRoark spotted some unwholesome relic, unrecognizable in its centuries of rust and decay—the peace remained. They walked back down to their camp, a third-hand tent they had bartered away from some drunken louts from Howth. The dark, ill-defined shapes VanRoark had sensed when Timonias had spoken to him again arose beneath his consciousness, but they were different, carrying with them more sadness than exultant triumph.

XVII

In all, they were at the Burn for about two weeks. Further tours of the army's main body revealed little other than that the riotous confusion was being constantly multiplied as men straggled in from the Barrens to the east or as more sailing ships dropped anchor in the clogged roadstead. A week after they arrived, a large tender, gray and somber as the fog banks from which she had silently emerged that morning, put into the anchorage, her scurrying brood of torpedo boats dashing around her at forty knots. The seabird and dolphin crests of the dead Dresau Islands were enameled on her bow, but she flew no flags other than the usual signal banners.

However, two things of real importance were discovered. First that Timonias was still on board his cancerously white ship, probably accompanied by whatever priests might have bothered to come to the Meadows. The cruiser was still close inshore, lying neither with the glut of wooden sailing ships nor with the ships from the rim nations clustered along the causeway.

Even compared to the infrequent stirrings of the steel ships, the merchant cruiser was a ghost ship; not once had VanRoark seen a single living person on her decks, a single wisp of steam escape from her funnel, a single flag hoisted in response to some shoreward signal. When he questioned someone on this seeming desertion, they would inevitably just smile and say that Timonias was on board and what more did one need to know?

He wondered if this lack of watchfulness had prompted the *Garnet's* men to make any expeditions for loot. But the barque was no longer at her anchorage and VanRoark quickly ceased to think about her.

The second thing was his rediscovery of Smythe. He had been walking westward along the no-man's-land between the rim nations and the army, toward the foot of the causeway and the parked aircraft. To his right, a wrecker crane had been drawn up alongside a large armored troop carrier; one of its engines had been removed and several men were working on it beside the tank. One of them was Smythe.

VanRoark moved over and watched quietly, remembering his clumsy conversation with the artilleryman just the other day. Eventually plates were secured again and torqued down; the wrecker lifted the engine over the open hatch and then lowered it gently from sight. Smythe turned from the vehicle, wiping oil from his blackened hands, and saw VanRoark.

He was smiling, obviously enjoying himself; VanRoark asked him under whose flag he had found such employment. They talked lightly for a while, walking down to the Sea under the long wings of the aircraft, their distorted reflections flowing on the aluminum and glass.

XVIII

The next two days VanRoark spent with Smythe and the men from a nation of which he had never heard. The things he used to feel and think at Sea when they had passed the ruins, or even back home when he had wandered along the Old Navy Dock, were remembered. The fears about exactly which army he had joined once again receded before the memory-forms of pilings and bollards that used to hold battle cruisers against the dock.

At dusk of the second day they walked along the causeway, over the drawbridge, and then westward almost a mile, so they could feel the rush of warm air as the aircraft landed or departed; the noise and vibration shook VanRoark and his mind. A violence he had never sensed rumbled within and sent him rising off the world with the green, tan and black mottled craft. When they came in very low over the Sea, over the anchored fleets, he could see their shockwaves rippling up from the water, crashing against the causeway, and then beginning again on the northern Sea.

Smythe told him again how ships like those, but infinitely greater, had once journeyed to the stars he now saw above the eastern horizon—but that was legend.

On the third day VanRoark could not find Smythe; none of the men he had been working with knew where he was, but VanRoark spent the day with them, pulling the turret from a tank and cleaning mechanisms whose workings he could not even guess at.

He finished sometime around six in the evening and left for his tent. One of the men suggested he move away from the army and into one of the rim nations' camps. "Hell, he's closer to those lovely tents where he is now," said another.

"Well, yeah," the first man grinned, "but I think the army's lads are getting a little restive, you know?"

VanRoark did not.

"Well, the whole army is just getting a little tense as far as we're concerned. They think our ships and machines are more the Devil's than their God's. And Timonias and his mates out on their ship don't seem to be helping the situation one way or the other. We need some help; those dudes have got us outnumbered at least a hundred to one and almost every night a couple of them come sneaking across the strip. Christ, most of this stuff's at least four hundred years old and shot to pieces with age and things we could never set straight. Now we got them cutting wires and dumping sand into the petrol. Just like the old days, they tell me; a few nights ago some of them tried to jump the crew of one of our destroyers, pirate her, for crissake!"

"What happened to them?"

The joker answered now: "They found out which ship they

came from, an old barque from Enador or someplace, and escorted her out to Sea. Our ship came back with a couple of empty shell casings and no more barque." A short laugh, and then much lower and more savage, "Stinking bastards, stinking pirating bastards!"

"That's part of it too, mate. A lot of the camp isn't too happy about friendly little sinkings like that. They're talking too much over there about things they don't understand."

VanRoark thanked them for the warning and walked slowly back to his tent, the army's lights and colors growing more sinister and menacing; now that he looked it did seem that a lot more attention was being paid to weapons than when they had first arrived. Gryfons were conspicuously draped in light mail and shod with steel-clawed slippers. It could not be that the army was moving on the Meadows, because then the rim nations would have known too. Besides, such an occasion would have been one for celebration and last feasts. This was entirely too businesslike. Most likely, though, it was only his imagination.

Tapp did not return that night and VanRoark assumed he was merely off on some particularly elaborate binge. He could not sleep and spent quite some time debating on whether the camp's quiet was normal or extraordinary. Around two in the morning he decided to try to find Tapp and ask him about what the army thought of the rim nations.

The camp did seem unusually quiet, but it was a broken, fractured quiet cut up only by the rough singing of drunken men. Between the songs of battle and love there was nothing, not even the wind from the Barrens. He looked south to the ruins of Brampton Hall, half expecting to see spectral lights and vapors hovering about them. *Working yourself up into a proper frenzy, VanRoark*, he thought.

When he couldn't find Tapp, VanRoark decided to look for Smythe. He passed through the sleeping army and across the strip to the rim nations. There too, the quiet was almost oppressive, but there was no drunken singing, only the sandy crunch of a patrol's boots.

He headed down to where he thought Smythe had his tent, near to the line of armored troop carriers where he had first spotted him.

The tent was set back toward the riverbank and it stank, for Smythe had been dead for more than a day; his throat had been slit and the blood had collected in the tent's waterproofed bottom, crusty and granular like the Burn's soil. VanRoark lit a small lamp that was hanging from the middle of the tent frame, and stared at the body. Even in his savage, brutal world, with death and the corpses of nations lying all around, he had never really seen a dead man. Most curious, it did look like Smythe, and the more he looked the more fascinated he became with the exposed arteries and collarbones; it had been a sloppy job.

Then he reached down to touch the dried blood and stiffened flesh; the eyes, which had followed the aircraft and sorted out their allegiance, were now gray and clouded. Smythe? He had been alive; now he stank. If any insects still lived in the Burn they would be boring into him, eating him.

VanRoark stared harder, his eyes starting to water and the top of his brain collapsing. New forms arose in his consciousness, indistinct but pulsing with anger and frustration. And wrapped up in the center of them was Yarrow, spitting his corroded lungs into the Sea. Why? No answer, but Yarrow was there with his holy books and a blade smelling of incense and olive oil.

VanRoark crawled out of the tent, his mind reeling and fighting with itself, wanting at once to get to Yarrow and then asking itself, *Why Yarrow? Why not one of the rim nations' men or one from the army itself? Or Tapp? Or suicide?* He had not even looked to see if Smythe had had a knife in his hands.

He was back in the middle of the army, gradually slowing down as the anger moved back from its first wild ravings. Anyway, Yarrow could be on board the cruiser with Timonias and the rest of the holy men. But then again, if he had done it to Smythe, in return for the beating he had got on the *Garnet*, then he still might be around. The beating and Smythe's apparent defection to the rim nations—that would have been enough to send Yarrow off the deep end.

Could he still be ashore, and if he was, how was he to be found among the army's millions? Inexplicably VanRoark began wondering if he was going through all this because he only thought that one should be properly outraged at the death of some man, or whether he felt any real anger over the death of the man who was Smythe. Why hadn't he alerted others in the camp? At least they might have helped in the search for Yarrow.

Because of the fumings and self-accusations going on within him, it was quite some time before he became aware of the sounds, smooth or sometimes rasping, but always cold and low. There were only a few isolated singers carrying on the drunken roaring of earlier in the evening. He thought he could pick up the words to "Brampton Hall," slurred and spotted with obscenities when they fit the rhyme.

He recognized the sound: moving metal, metal being drawn across leather or whetting stone or more metal. Almost like the Sea, except for the occasional, musical pingings when someone got clumsy. Rough and pitted metal, grinding like sand or Burn soil; fresh, oiled, and polished, moving like silk against silk, its sound smooth and brocaded in the air.

This did not fit in at all. VanRoark was quite at a loss to find room for this in his preoccupation with Yarrow, so he tried to disregard it.

He walked quickly, ignoring the swelling raspings and his lack of destination. He heard the singing grow louder too and soon spotted a man staggering down the deserted avenue. It was Tapp and he hailed him.

VanRoark ran up to the little man and asked if he had seen Yarrow in the past few days. Tapp was largely insensitive to this, having trouble remembering anyone named Yarrow at all. "Why?" he asked drunkenly, his grinning face less than a foot from VanRoark's.

" 'Cause I think he killed Smythe!" VanRoark was dimly aware of how hysterical he sounded; somehow he was proud of this, for he thought it was the right state in which to be.

Tapp looked at him stupidly. Then a smile of forced recognition spread over his dark features. VanRoark got ready for some predictable graveyard humor about Smythe's mother or comparative worth in life. "Oh yeah . . ." Tapp crooned, lifting his right hand.

The middle of Tapp's face disappeared, nose and upper

jaw; his lower jaw flopped down against his throat while his yellowed eyes bulged from their untouched sockets.

VanRoark thought the older man's expression unbelievably funny, like an ape trying to mimic human disbelief. The younger man looked back into the eyes and felt himself laughing along with Tapp at his marvelous joke; how wonderful to have a wit that could make a man's death and one's self-appointed vengeance the object of laughter. Lord, how stupid he had made himself look, how utterly brainless, with just a big dark hole gaping between his eyes and trapeze jaw. VanRoark saw that one of Tapp's wisdom teeth was badly impacted.

He vaguely suspected he was thinking all this in the space of less than half a second. It was ended as a faint popping noise reached his ears, and then the razor edge of Tapp's strangled breath cut through his mind, searching for a tongue with which to scream. Blood, dark and oily in the false dawn and torchlight, burst from the wound with astounding force, splattering against VanRoark's tunic, and then was smeared as Tapp tottered forward and fell against him.

VanRoark stepped back from the writhing creature, with its knife shrieks so low he could hardly hear them over the sliding metal and the bubbling of its blood.

VanRoark's mind was a confused blank now, a vacuum like that found in the center of an explosion, a storming, uncontrollable nothing that could do nothing but try to explode some more. VanRoark began his own yelling, trying to shut out the sound and even the sight of Tapp. He began kicking at the body, stamping on it to make it stop living or at least to have it make some human scream, some evidence of human agony. It only turned and twisted in the ground-glass soil, the sharp, gurgling sounds still creeping into VanRoark's ears.

Around him, the sliding noises were increasing as were the poppings. They took on power and definition, became loud and vicious.

Tapp's body moved away from him, but it could have been VanRoark who was moving, running through the suddenly living army. His vision was clouded and tinged with red, but he could still see the men spilling out of the tents. The sound of metal against metal was that of shells being rammed into breeches, swords being drawn from scabbards, weapons being assembled—now all in the hands of the army —and the thousand torches that burst into flame.

VanRoark slammed into some men, kept running, his direction determined only by which of his random, flailing movements met with the least resistance. He understood none of this.

Booming, inhuman wailings came to him from the anchorage. He thought that Tapp had found a way to scream. Then he broke free of the tents facing the Sea and saw that it was the sirens of the steel ships calling to each other.

He blundered out into the Sea, knee-deep, and then ran, fell, and crawled back onto the beach. In front of him the army was burning: the flames, the madmen, with their war axes weaving in and out of the torch-fires until he could not tell them apart, hurled themselves outward from the center of the camp, gathering fury as they spiraled outward.

The line of savagery gathered up its southern end as it reached the mountains below Brampton Hall, then turned back and joined the north, crashing into the encampments of the rim nations.

VanRoark staggered down the beach, drawn inward by the suction of the brutal flood. He fell again, the army spinning around him, alternating with the Sea, where the ships were beginning to stir. Steam escaped from their hulls and stacks with more hideous screeching, metallic. Diamond searchlights flared on their towers, sweeping the wooden fleets as maggot crews scurried under their brilliance. A sane part of VanRoark struggled to make itself heard before it was utterly swallowed by madness and the shattering night; the army was destroying itself: it was murdering the rim nations.

He spun around: Brampton Hall was burning in the reflected light of the army. Again, and the northern limits of the Burn were in front of him; aircraft, some on fire or with tiny figures clinging to their skins, trying to plunge javelins through them.

The roaring of the battle now became more jagged as the

rim nations finally wakened themselves to what was actually happening. VanRoark could see sheets of red-yellow lifting upward and south from where the great lines of field guns were; then dying down, but still burning, for they had not even had enough time to pull the tarpaulins from their barrels. The wall, again, as they fired fragmentation shells set to burst thirty feet from the muzzles.

Rapid chatterings of automatic cannon and machine guns, great, brutal detonations and shockwaves beat his head into the sand as the ships began firing into the wooden fleets or shoreward at the army.

He could no longer hear himself, and he could not tell whether it was because the noise was too great or the middle of his face had been shot off and his voice lost with it.

Huge, infinitely vicious rhythms shook and kicked him, driving him first into the shallows and then lifting him back toward the rim nations. *Am I still walking or have my legs also been shot away and the concussion hurling me through the air?*

He felt the airplanes struggling up from the causeway and then turning, some so low they set ships afire and the Sea boiling with their fire-wake; he looked up and saw the bombs falling like ripe, clustered fruit from their wings, as from the limbs of trees. The acetylene light of phosphorus and the billowing, morbidly luxurious clouds of Greek fire and jellied gasoline rose from the army's camp.

The massed artillery on the tanker's decks opened together and a quarter square mile of men disappeared where the shells hit. Everything, everywhere his eye was forced, were fires, fires of every color he had ever imagined or seen on the flags of the army: turquoise and deep opal to blue to white to a hell-blackness from burnings so hot they had no time or energy to squander on ordinary light. Things leaping, being blown into the air, moving as their lives splattered out of them, their limbs blasted away from them as they fell; then more fires and detonations to drive them into the Burn, pounding them into it, breaking their shrieking agony like a sledgehammer against a mirror.

He began running; he still had legs, he thought with a

mind that had long since been forced outside of its skull by the weight of the chaos crashing down around him.

He stumbled into the camp, avenues faced and walled with fire. The noise compressed around him, suffocating, collapsing his bones and shoving his eyes into flat disks, fish eyes. All around, running shapes, men who should not have been running, carrying parts of themselves in their hands, trophies of their holy struggle; the sand was slick and glittering with fresh blood and the garbage-shreddings of men.

VanRoark lost all orientation; even the thunderous salvos from the rim nations' batteries or from their ships in the roadstead offered no guide, for they seemed to be all around him. Dark, jerking shapes, tanks or even the serpentine forms of the land trains drove though the fires, their howling sirens, guns and engines rising and then falling as they fled.

A pressure, heated far past any temperature, gripped his arm below the shoulder and rested there for a split second; then, when it had burned its way into the bone, pulled.

VanRoark screamed; for a moment he heard himself and nothing else and spun to see his right arm pinwheeling away from him, turning red, then orange, then blue, then white, as it passed in front of and through the fires.

The wound does not seem to hurt, his mind gibbered to itself; *no, but now I am torn open and through this, all the fury of the battle will pour into me; I will be lost.* The violence erupted inside him; he could *see* the explosions and burning silk of his disintegrating organs.

There is nothing left of me, nothing left but a pierced skin separating one segment of the hell from another.

He saw a man moving like a puppet or character in a badly animated film, from the strobe-light effect of the infinite explosions surrounding him. He was dazed, his eyes clouded to the point of appearing as gray blanks; only his mouth held any sign of emotion, and that was bitterness. He was dressed in the remains of an olive uniform and carried a large pack on his back; from it a dragon's spine of machine gun bullets ran over his shoulder and down into the weapon he was holding. The barrel guard had been lost and the metal was glowing cherry red. The steam from his melting hand drifted around the barrel and joined with the cloud of powder smoke spurting from the muzzle. An unbroken line of green phosphorus tracers streamed from the man and the gun, blanketing and momentarily silencing the rest of the battle, like a hose spraying molten metal onto a blaze.

As the man walked by and above VanRoark, he struggled to his feet, possessed by the idea that he must speak to the man: ask him about his numberless self-deceptions for coming to the Meadows; about the artificial arm he must get when the other had turned to slag; about his barques and battle cruiser and the books in his library.

VanRoark made it but not before the man had almost disappeared into the battle-haze. His voice was lost again; he picked up a broken sword hilt, a severed hand still gripping it fanatically, and threw the lot of it at the man to attract his attention.

Slowly, easily, the man turned back to VanRoark, the smoking green line of shells fanning out from him, swinging around without break or interruption, coming closer, becoming a single planet of green that was transformed to a star filling VanRoark's eyes.

VanRoark fell once again. This time it had been the side of his skull, the right side, that had been ripped apart; he thought he could see the eye rolling away from him, the stump of the optic nerve slapping the ground like a piece of wet gristle.

Ludicrously (it must have been so because he could remember laughing aloud at it) part of his sight seemed to remain with the liberated eye ball. He could see himself, the bloody ruin of his face and the stump of his right arm; and the two eyes calmly, coldly, regarded each other and passed judgment on their relative situations.

He thought it even funnier when, through all the smoke of violence, a gull settled down in front of his right eye. The creature, living in the wilderness, had become too hungry to ignore a feast such as the army was serving up.

VanRoark howled with delight as he thought he could feel the bird take the nerve stump in its beak and rise into the air. He saw his own body, matted and mired with blood, and then more bodies as the bird gained height;

then men fighting and a vehicle crashing imperiously through their private war for salvation.

An aircraft shot under his eye, loosed its rolling mass of napalm, silhouetting its bat-wings; then it exploded, falling to earth and exploding again.

He could see almost the whole of the Burn and most of the roadstead, split and scarred with the wrecks of ships and the frantic wakes of torpedo boats. Everything grew diffuse and indistinct; colors expanded and drifted suddenly in impossible ways; encrustations of black and white fires, green tracers and fragmentation shells laced through the Burn's glowing darkness and the Sea. He could see the army collapsing in upon itself, dissolving into its own fire and panic.

A random spray of tracer shells, orange this time, moved upward. He sensed the pressure of the gull's beak lessen and then end entirely. His eye hurtled back down into the Burn, the colors rushing away from a black center, their vague forms becoming vicious shards. Then he saw the inside of the lightless fires and watched, as from yet a third eye, as his vision melted and was splattered all through it.

XIX

There was pain, a great deal of it, and blurred streakings of light that were ebon at their centers, white along the bodies and then refracted into rainbow edgings as they drove into the empty eye socket and ricocheted through his skull.

He could recall the background against which the lights moved turning from black to cobalt to silver and then back again; he could recall the sharp soil of the Burn grinding underneath him, how it sparkled in the reflections from the lights. Then it would become damp and hard; small, penitent waves would wash up against him. The salt stung in his wounds but they felt cleaner when they had been washed.

He moved away from the Sea and through the ruins of the camp; the vague and shadowed impressions were now punctuated with single details, unusually sharp against the formations of color; that was mostly gray now. Charred poles and family standards passed above him, their faces and wrought designs torn and brutalized.

He had thought the machines different from the men, with their filth and tattooed arms. But both had apparently died in the same ways: the smooth skins were bitten into by cold or flaming metal, wrenched away from the skeletons, and the guts of plastic or copper or blood or brain would be knocked loose, spilling through the wound like vomit from a drunk's mouth. The debris dried where it caught on the skin or poured upon the ground. He crept past a tank which had excreted its crew through a gaping hole in its forward parts; in turn, the concussion had torn the crew apart, allowing their own interiors to partially escape them..

A piece of silk, embroidered with swords and basilisks, came into his left eye; it was still flying proud and upright, pathetically arrogant to the wreckage that lay all around it.

Slivers of gray rested in the roadstead behind him. All that was left of the wooden fleets was a tangle of splintered masts, burned flags and rigging. A few shapes, silver or dull green, were piled up on the causeway.

Were they all dead? There was no sound, not even the crunch of sand or some victorious cry from the seabirds as they moved from one meal to another. Nothing: only his breathing, sharp and edged like broken glass—like Tapp's had been.

After the background had shifted from light to dark and back again several times, it abruptly became a flat gray that never changed; a noise finally worked back into his mind, a low purring as vague and ill-defined as the shapes that had moved before him.

The gaping hollowness in him, which had allowed the fires and then the charred silence to move freely in his body, was demarcated by a single bright coil of wire. Then a straight line and more coils until they defined the emptiness with their tapestries. They pulled the edges of the wounds together; the humming grayness was not shut out entirely now, but it was split up and filtered through the wires.

A strange coldness welled out from the spiders' webs. Colors began reconstructing themselves in the blank spaces between the sound and wires. Cautiously, feeling crept back into the web-works where his eye and arm had been; the colors moved in with it. The pain had almost died by now except for short eruptions that compacted the light into nothing. The cold became comforting to him even when the pain was nearly forgotten.

XX

The trouble with building from the webs was that he always had to begin with them, for there was nothing else; when he opened his eye to the uniform gray of the world he could see wire profiles of men moving in front of him. In time, the profiles became three-dimensional as more wires conformed to the shapes of faces and limbs.

The colors he had seen when he was blind now moved outward and fastened to the external frameworks, set, shifted, and reset.

He was in a room about eight feet square and seven feet high. It was the uniform gray of unpainted metal, featureless except for a washbasin in the near corner, a door set in the wall opposite to where he lay, and a metal cabinet that might have been a desk; neat welds joined the metal panels of the compartment. There was a window, he thought, on the wall next to his bunk; but he could only see a wavering slice of dawnlight playing up and down on the door.

VanRoark looked down with his left eye toward a plaster wrapped right arm; he should have lost that. He could feel bandages covering the space where his right eye should have been. A very slight motor vibration could be felt through the walls and the whole room itself sometimes bounced unexpectedly. Presently a man entered; he was tall and fairly old, probably in his early sixties. He wore a tan blouse and trousers that once might have been the uniform of some nation. He was bald, white hairs growing thinly on the side of his rounded, heavy skull.

He looked at VanRoark briefly; the younger man tried to speak but found that he could not. The man opened the desk cabinet and unrolled two flexible cables; their heads were snapped into sockets on a metal plate set into the plaster cast. For the first time, VanRoark felt warmth in the space where his arm had been; it poured upward, flowing past his shoulder and then outward to fill his whole body.

The madness of the wire frames evaporated. VanRoark fell asleep, a dark, soft burrow in which there were no dreams, no struggling colors, nothing but the warmth and rest.

"You've been out for quite a while; almost three months." The bald man's voice was deep, but not quite as deep as Tapp's had been; VanRoark noticed that his jaw had not moved when he spoke the words. "How do you feel?"

"Fine," a voice croaked; VanRoark supposed it was his.

"You hardly look it, friend. You came very close to dropping off completely, you know." VanRoark nodded that he did.

There was a moment of awkward silence. "Look, my name's Cavandish. I'd shake hands with you and all but I can see you're a little inconvenienced."

"Amon VanRoark, sir."

"Then, Amon, I guess you wonder exactly what is going on here." Cavandish looked embarrassed with himself at this. "Damn, I can't help falling into stupid understatements and clichés. At least I've relieved you of the responsibility of saying 'Where am I?' "

VanRoark tried to smile. "All right, where am I?"

Cavandish chuckled politely. "Right then. You're on a land train heading east. You see, when the army broke up, we had a lot of trouble getting out and . . ."

The thin smile faded from the old man's immobile jaw. "No one knows. It just looked like the army suddenly took it into its head that the rim nations were either defiling the purity of their mission with their ships and tractors, or maybe they even thought that we were the army of Evil and they could save themselves the walk to the Meadows by getting us then and there.

"I really don't know about it, Amon. I've been told of the armies surviving the Meadows, even after being momentarily defeated by whatever showed up under the Opposition's flag; but I've never heard of anything like this—this suicide. The bastards just turned on us." The tone of voice was still fairly calm, but VanRoark noticed that the man was methodically grinding one fist into a meathook palm. "Oh, by the Lord, we gave them a proper fight. No Abstractions, no allegiances to Good or Evil or any garbage about ending the world, just a good honest round of murdering and finally a chance to face those bastards who'd been slowly sucking the rim nations white. Right in their stinking faces."

Cavandish sighed helplessly. "Well, anyway, we were just about the last vehicle out of the Burn. Lord! You should've seen the bodies. I'd never imagined that the army could have attracted so many men until I saw the dead. Thousands! Millions, for all I know. It sounded like someone popping popcorn, with the tires grinding up their bones.

"We were just getting clear of the mountains, trying to keep up with the only other train to make it out and a couple of fast tanks, when something set off the real fuel carts. So while Maus and I tried to get them unhooked and rolling back into the Burn before they really touched off, the rest of our informal group scattered.

"Things got a little dodgy then because the train's power linkages were all fouled up from the battle. We dragged ourselves out along the ridges and set down in back of some ruins."

"Brampton Hall?"

"If that's what it's called. Mainly, we just hid up there, letting go a few discreet rounds once in a while when it looked like something unfriendly might be trying to climb out of that bone heap to get at us. By the third day we had the train fixed up and we also found you. Christ, man! You looked dreadful, like Death himself crawling up to get us. Maus wanted to put you out of it right there, but Kenrick, doctor to the last, loaded you up and patched you together as best he could."

"There are others here?"

"There were five, but Maus took a dart just as we were pulling away from those ruins and the poison got to him. Lyndir and Zaccaharias got the fever about a month ago, from vampire bats, Kenrick said. Corwin died when we ran into a mounted patrol going home to Mountjoy. And poor old Kenrick just went mad one day, started muttering all kinds of stuff about springtime and a girl named Gold or something. I found a note later saying he was going Home—he capitalized it, like it was a country or something—and that was the last I knew of him." Cavandish shook his great head slowly. "Ah, poor old Kenrick, you might have enjoyed him, Amon."

VanRoark felt the silence descend again. "Were we the only ones to make it out of the Burn? Did they get all of the rim nations?"

He waited a second before Cavandish roused himself. "Almost," the old man drawled slowly, sadly. "A lot of the regular army got off, but I suspect they had taken care to leave before the shooting started. But no, they didn't get us all. I was up in that Hall of yours, watching them while Maus and Zaccaharias worked on the train, but—and somehow this makes me feel good—we just scattered." He threw his arms apart, fingers almost touching the walls of the small cabin. "I guess some headed back home; others just ran out of fear, but still more out of disgust. Amon, I could see the faces of those men as they rode out of the Burn; I've never seen such bitterness. Man, all they wanted to do was run! Run so fast that the only thing they could taste would be their own blood when their lungs burst or when their planes had crushed them flat with the acceleration.

"And I could see that others were moving out to the north, to the Meadows. About seven planes made it off the causeway and five of them headed north. Some torpedo boats and even one of the smaller destroyers managed to get under that bridge and they followed the aircraft. I could see dust trails of trucks and tanks and motor artillery moving north, stopping as they forded the river and then starting up again on the other side."

VanRoark looked up to the old man; his face was the color of copper ore. "Are we headed for the Meadows, sir?"

"No." Cavandish stared out the window that VanRoark could not see; he rubbed his hands over his eyes. "No. We're going east now, to Blackwoods Bay."

"But Cynibal's wiped out; there was a war."

"I'm going there to find some fuel, trying to get enough to get me home." Cavandish glanced slowly around the room and then returned his eyes to VanRoark. "Did any of the men you might have talked to, men from the rim nations, tell you why they were there at the Burn, and why they wanted to die?"

VanRoark remembered Yarrow first because he had offered the loudest and most involved explanations for his conduct; then Smythe and Tapp, moving back and forth uncertainly between God, the Devil, and Brampton Hall. He remembered the artilleryman with the armored Death on his forearm. "They said they were tired."

"And that, Amon, is what I am. I came to the Meadows because, somehow, it promised peace. And a flaming lot of that it gave me! Traveled for five years to get there, and for what? To see my finest friends shot to pieces or catch some godawful disease that let them bleed to death on the inside; to see the last shining bits of metal my nation and others had hoarded away for this single moment destroyed by the same pack of bastards that had been out to get us before any holy missions had ever been proclaimed.

"Christ, Amon, if they want to fight at the Meadows after what was done to them, then I salute them because they've a lot more patience than I do. At this moment I am sick of everything! I just want to move with my train, just move and never really be anyplace." Cavandish thought this over for a second and then decided to be amused with himself. "Ravings of an old man, Amon. We'll see you tomorrow and get you out of bed." Cavandish unplugged the cables from his cast and reeled them back into the cabinet.

The color faded from Cavandish's image and the skin dissolved from his face to reveal the wire framework; the room was reduced to a gray monotone, outlined and supported by single threads of drawn metal. Then even the wires unreeled back into someplace beyond VanRoark's perception and he guessed that he slept.

VanRoark awakened to the same sequence of wire frameworks and growing colors, but now it was quicker and more like simply opening his eyes. He saw that Cavandish had attached two more tubes to his cast; he felt curiously whole and ready to start getting around again.

As he waited for the old man, he thought about his arm in the cast, absolutely sure he had seen it shot off; strangely, he thought the space where his right eye had been felt filled instead of empty with vaporous blood. Then there was Cavandish himself; VanRoark liked the man already, but why had his jaw not once moved all the while he was speaking to him?

Cavandish came in, disconnected the tubes and told VanRoark to get up; that he was all right for the moment. For a second, as he rose, the colors blurred into the monotone and their wire skeletons reemerged, stark and shining against the gray. Then the wire was overlaid with liquid flowings; he was standing up, Cavandish smiling tiredly at his side.

They moved unsurely through the door and then turned left, walking down a narrow corridor past three similar doors; all were dogged shut. At the end of the corridor was another door, this one on the right, and VanRoark could feel cool evening breezes drifting through it.

"All right, now. There's a ladder right below the combing and from there it's about ten feet to the ground. Watch that cast, and tell me if you think you can make it." VanRoark grasped a railing on the outside of the corridor wall and swung himself outboard until he could find the first rungs. He was quite surprised at the near absence of pain and his strength.

"How long have I been out?" he cried up to Cavandish.

"About four months. It's winter now up north, you know."

VanRoark was not ready for this and almost lost his balance. When he banged his cast into the steel wall of the car he did not feel any real discomfort.

He stepped off the ladder and looked up and down the length of the land train. To his left, to the east he judged from the sun, were three cars like his own, painted a dull sand and olive. They were essentially just boxes, unpierced on this side save for ventilator slits, about forty feet long and perhaps twenty feet thick. Two wheels, each at least twelve feet in diameter, supported each side of the box. Forward of these cars was the control vehicle; this was much larger, twice the size of the passenger cars. A sheet of glass, canted outward about ten degrees, wound around the forward edge of the car. There was a railing bordering the stepped, two-level roof of the car. An artillery piece, draped in heavy canvas, was mounted near the forward edge of the car's roof.

To VanRoark's right was one more of the boxlike cars and then about six slightly bulged cars. The analogy of a huge wheeled serpent was unavoidable.

"Like her?" Cavandish was on the ground next to him.

"And you run all of this, alone?" VanRoark asked in amazement.

"So far. It's been kind enough not to present me with any difficulties that'd require a Zaccaharias or a Maus to fix. About the most troublesome operation has been you, Amon, and Kenrick seems to have fixed that up well enough for me to fumble through. I'm taking off your bandages after dinner."

"No period of recuperation or anything like that?"

Cavandish laughed politely. "Hardly; you've had four months of that. Kenrick figured it'd be easier for me if you did your healing in one spot and quietly. You'll have to be careful for a while, though; some of your muscles might have atrophied despite the doctor's drugs."

It was beginning to get dark. VanRoark could see a star or two appearing over the control car's gun. They moved over to a small fire, where Cavandish had some coffee and a skewered jackeroo heating. They ate in comparative silence, the old man apparently having nothing more to say for the moment and VanRoark suddenly concerned only with getting some solid food into his stomach. He did not realize just how much it had shrunk, and was gorged after only a few bites.

When they finished, Cavandish brought a small leather case out and drew closer to VanRoark. "Now, you know that you're, ah, different than you were before the army broke up," he began cautiously.

"You mean my arm and eye?" VanRoark asked. "I was sure they had been shot off."

"They were, but Kenrick replaced them with mechanical substitutes which I assure you are almost the equals of your original limbs, maybe even superior in some areas. Now, I'm telling you this before I take off the bandages because some people get fairly worked up when they take a first look at a new arm or leg. These aren't just hooks or pegs, Amon; you have an arm that will feel everything your old one could, move in every direction your old one could. You have a small lens setup where your right eye used to be; it'll pipe images directly into the brain just as the first eye did. And even better; you'll be seeing more with this one. You can adjust the range to see into the far ends of the spectrum, far past the limits where light radiation becomes invisible X-rays or simple heat."

Cavandish considered this for a moment and then decided it was not enough. "Look, I think I know how you'll feel because I felt the same way myself. You see, my lower jaw and larynx were pretty well torn up by shell fragments down on the Burn. Kenrick fitted me up with a whole artificial jaw and all I need to eat and speak. That's why I don't move my jaw much—because it's riveted to my skull."

"And what did this Kenrick have? Was he all of flesh and blood?" VanRoark was amazed at the tinges of bitterness which edged into his voice.

"Ah, Kenrick. No; before we left our home he had this operation and got a mechanical heart; some of the motor areas of his brain were solid state electronics too.

"Enough talk. Here, give me your arm and we'll show that it isn't so bad after all." Cavandish cut away his shirt, almost apologetically it seemed, and then began making a long incision on the side of the shoulder and arm cast with a knife that hummed like the grayness. "All right," he said when he was through, "here it comes." He gave a slight tug and the cast fell apart into five pieces.

VanRoark gazed down at where the stump of his shoulder was neatly tucked into a blued steel collar; the skin was drawn and slightly wrinkled around the collar as if someone had carefully riveted and then shrunk the serrated ring around the arm—which was probably just what had been done anyway. From the ring, which looked like a bracelet, proceeded an arm such as one could find on the armored dress of the Great Plains knights. Finally, there was a hand —or rather a gauntlet, for the fingers were hinged and a flaring skirt of metal hid the wrist joint.

He held the hand up to his left eye; it was engraved, even to the palm, and the hunting parties and serpents ran down from the shoulder ring in a parade such as he had only seen in the tapestries of his home cathedral. There was a small sun in the center of his hand, and tiny planets with continents of gunmetal and seas of silver spinning around it. Galaxies patterned the metal folds of the hand, clustering in thick bands that cut in back of the solar system, random agglomerations filling in the cobalt spaces between, and then fading out into the wrist and fingers. There was a rocket, long and barbed with graceful wings, one side etched in bare silver light from the silver sun; it was bound outward. There was a serpent, winged with almost as much grace, coiled about his index finger; a lance whose grip and guard solidified out of the universe dust ran nearly the length of the middle finger. Finally, there was a man, a knight in fine-etched mail, on his fourth finger—and a queen on his last finger whose hair was wound around the metal like the body of the dragon.

Cavandish looked a little embarrassed at all this. "Please don't be honored, Amon; none of that was done for you," he said, almost laughing. "The arm is as old as the train, maybe older, and was used by many men before it came to you. Some of them were artists and naturally spent some time dressing it up."

"Dead men's arm?" VanRoark asked absently.

"Well, if you want to be morbid about it, I suppose it is." VanRoark did not hear this, for his eye was traveling up the length of the arm, over the lines of rune figures and numbers and even some formulae, over forests seeded with all manner of fantastic animals, unicorns, hippogriffs, hooded-basilisks and gryfons—cut by roads and cities that spiraled upward around mountains, their streets awash in swarming crowds of etched figures, their battlements and gates proud against skies where the galaxies once again appeared. There were ships upon his arm, fine great sailing craft and steel battle cruisers, no less powerful for their microscopic length.

VanRoark moved the arm unsurely, expecting to hear it creak or feel the hideous scrape of metal against bone within him; but none of that happened. He felt only the cool of the evening air upon it, and when he laid the metal palm to the sandy ground he could feel the rough granules—even a slight twinge of pain as he brushed over a piece of dead thornbush.

He touched himself; the metal was as warm as his skin, but its strength and rigidity was indisputably that of steel.

Cavandish saw him smiling too. "Ah, good, now for your eye." He raised his tool and began to work on the cast. "Keep your eye closed."

"Huh?"

"Keep it closed; even the firelight might be something of a shock after so long." VanRoark shrugged and commanded a lid he was sure did not exist to close; he was almost happy when he felt nothing move.

The cast was removed and VanRoark was further reassured when he couldn't see a thing out of where his right eye had been. "Not a thing, sir."

"Of course not, you've got it closed. Open it."

The younger man blinked his left eye and then tried to repeat the muscle sequence on the right side of his face. There were wires before him again, or rather woolen threads whose color was solid only in their centers and then diffused off into the darkness. The color mists shifted and expanded; he could see the campfire in front of him. "It'll take a little time for everything to sort itself out."

"Who owned *this* before me?"

"No one at all; now is the time to be honored. Honored not only for the eye but for the incredible job Kenrick did of weaving it into the stump of your optic nerve. A really incredible feat for a man in his condition. There's a small metal plate around it where some bone used to be, so don't worry if you feel the skin pulling a little when you smile or scream or, something. And try not to touch the lens—it protrudes a little—feel it?—because it's fairly easy to smudge or get dirtied up. And watch your right hand; you could easily forget it's not entirely human and put a scratch onto it." Cavandish settled back and watched VanRoark for a while; he decided not to mention the grotesque effect the lens tube made twisting in and out of the skull plate as VanRoark focused to different distances.

"What makes it run?"

"Body enzymes, the natural electrical impulses of your own nervous system. Kenrick could have told you more. He knew all about men."

"And you know nothing by comparison?"

Cavandish answered good-humoredly. "I am but a poor simple navigator carrying out the instructions of a wise and learned man of healing."

"Ah, a navigator." VanRoark's attention was easily diverted, for now he had already ceased to notice any difference between the functioning of his real and artificial limbs. "You've always been with the land train, then?"

Cavandish considered a moment and then chose to follow the drift of the conversation. "No, not always."

"Then what did you do before the train? Where did your family come from?"

"From there." Cavandish pointed to the welkin. "From that part of the sky approximately, though I can no longer name the star, things have changed so much."

VanRoark really had no idea of what to say to this. The old man continued: "Though not originally, of course. The way I was told it, my family had left the world back in the days of the First World, or very soon after its end, when things were still going just about as they should have been.

"We are supposed to have spread out along the arms of our galaxy, searching around the numberless suns and finding an occasional world that was green and empty."

There were great pauses between each sentence, and longer ones before VanRoark spoke; it was as if the one was trying desperately to remember the proper questions while the other was slowly dredging up the answers from where they had laid for so long. "Why did they, your family, come back?"

Cavandish sighed. "They came back for the Wars; they all came back, all of the families who had left. It took a long time—which I suppose is why some of the rim nations seem so odd and out of touch with the current state of the world—but one by one, on every world where we had settled, the prophets appeared. And they spoke, these prophets, and we both know how they spoke, the words and the hope—how odd to call what they offered, *hope*—and we came back. All the sciences and beliefs that had lived for a bit longer on worlds named after stars and in countries named after gods . . . they came home. Of course, by this time, home was already degenerating into what it is now.

"But they—we tried, Amon, you'll have to give us that. We landed and founded the new nations that were only supposed to last for a few years, and we built our new machines and began, my great-grandfather told me, with such fine and noble purpose to play our part in all of this.

"Then the systems broke down, at time so ludicrously and utterly that even my proud, unbending fathers could not ignore it. We had lost our ships by then and the skill to steer them through the skies. The rim nations became scattered; some met their planned annihilation at the Meadows. Many, I suspect, were overrun by earthly enemies." Then his lips curled slightly upward, which was as close as Cavandish could come to a smile. "The men we had come so far to help in our mutual destiny hunted us out, and one by one they infected, sabotaged, betrayed the rim nations until all that was left was what you saw on the Burn."

The lips relaxed back into a scar line; VanRoark thought he could see wire mesh behind it. "Why?"

"Why did they destroy us?"

"Yes"—now VanRoark could feel himself smiling sadly—"us."

"For as many reasons as they had for coming to the Burn. Though mostly it seemed to us they hated the machines, the building. None of us could ever really figure it out completely. It was almost as if they just gave up being humans; they were more like the mindless, drifting forces that seem to be controlling the universe these days. They shift and flow and anything that is thrown up in their way—no matter if it is there for Good or Evil—anything that the rim nations shaped and built against the darkness, they hated. They hated the trucks and tractors which could have ended their starvation, the ships that could have ended their wandering."

There was silence then except for the fire and an odd, faint cracking that slowly grew louder. The pebbles and rocks of the wastes, heated during the day, were now cooling too quickly with the fall of night and shattering. VanRoark imagined it to be the huge, malicious applause of the world, complimenting Cavandish on the depth of his bewilderment and frustration.

"What did you build?" Why had he asked that?

At this a roaring laughter slipped out of Cavandish's knife-slit mouth; he looked like a ventriloquist's doll whose real voice was coming from somewhere else. "Me? Not me, Amon. Now, my grandfather, he was a builder; he worked in the shipyards repairing aircraft carriers and merchantmen. And my dad built bridges all the hell over the world—every single one of which was cut down or blown up within a year or two of its completion.

"I, on the other hand, am almost as much a child of this world as the army was; maybe even more so. I was a navigator-bombardier." Cavandish was laughing so hard that he had to stop talking and rub his jaws that had never moved. "I sat in the glass noses of our aircraft, like the big ones you saw on the causeway at the Burn.

"It was good for a while, you know. Because I could sit there alone with all the stars and a ribbon of black asphalt captured in the wire frame of the nose. Then, way off behind you, you'd hear the engines and feel the back of your seat pressing against you. Little dabs of white—no, it was more of a pale green in the starlight—moved under me and the plane until they blurred together.

"There were about ten, twenty seconds, just after we lifted off, while the landing gear was stowed, and that was like a tanner's hawk getting ready to fall or rise. The field was built beside a river and we had to fly down this valley for a few minutes; the engines were throttled back so we didn't clout some mountain and it was quite beautiful with the lights along the banks and maybe even some power-boats moving against the current.

"Then we were clear, over the Sea, and Pena would shove everything up against the pegs. Man, you should see the sky when we had to break through some clouds. You couldn't hear the engines at all up there; just like you were a little man sitting inside someone else's skull, with all the darkness around you except for the eye and its wire frame.

"I kept wanting to reach through the eye and grab the lights, especially the one my family had come back from—I knew which one it was then. But I remember that once I touched the glass and my skin froze to it, so I could only watch.

"But the watching was fair enough, in that eye. I have to laugh at myself now; I was young then, and I had given those skies to a woman, because I loved her, and in those days I still thought I owned the sky—whether from inheritance or default from the world I could never say." Cavandish closed his eyes and smiled faintly, and laughed as he said he must, very low and gently.

The eyes opened and were hard. "Pena would eventually come back and say that we were nearing the target. We dropped below the clouds and I couldn't see the stars anymore. I saw instead some dusty plain or plateau, or maybe a coastline where the surf was like a white line of pus trying to keep the land from infecting the Sea.

"Our formation, there were usually about four of us, would make one low run to make sure we had the right target; and then one more single line, stepped formation, if they couldn't throw anything up at us; from four different directions, one after the other, if they could."

"What did you bomb?"

"Ruins mostly. You see—I wonder if I will laugh at this too—when the nations came back, they built their cities and then left or were destroyed. Many of the ruins from the first days—when everything was going straight and no one had left for the sky—a lot of those are still half-alive. Like the Black Libraries, they still held invaluable machineries and knowledge."

"And you bombed this?" *This is like a minstrel show,* thought VanRoark, *with me as the straight man and Cavandish cracking the long, wretched jokes, and even the applause of the stupidly delighted audience in the crackling desert.*

"We had to. My fathers built many of them, but the world had grown too large and malignant for my poor rim nations. You see, many of these ruins which we had built or maintained for a while were then beyond our reach. They were in the hands of the world and they could only have hurt us. I know what you're going to cry to me now; about the knowledge in which all those godforsaken slobs might have found some measure of solace. Sure, we knew that, and we also flaming well knew that they would discard or warp or bungle anything that wouldn't suit their own vicious ends. That's what my grandfather found out when they loaded up an ancient ship they found moored in some northern river with equally ancient cordite they'd dug out of the Armories, and sailed it into his precious shipyard. And my father found out when they cut the suspension cables on one of his new bridges while he was still on it.

"All that we had left were the guns and the bombs. We couldn't get to the books or the machines or the art before the world did. So I sat behind the wired eye and looked through another one where there were only two wires, and when the Library or the church was under their intersection, I pressed a button. The bombs fell; sometimes I could see a bit of star or moonlight on their casings and fins.

"Then Pena would take us up and back to the stars and the river with the landing field beside it, the lights, and the hangars cut into the side of the valley walls.

"There were about forty bombers and a couple of dozen lighter craft operating from that field when I was still flying. As things went on, quite a few of them left for the Meadows and others just dropped apart from sheer exhaustion. Others crashed or were shot down or sabotaged, but mostly it was fuel. It came from Blackwoods Bay and every year there was less and less of it. Then they started sinking the tankers or fouling up the oil, even when we sent escort ships along. Finally, there was that nice little war that Ihetah and Cynibal decided to have.

"So gradually there were fewer craft lifting off. And, oh, you should have seen the lads who still kept flying. Lord! How grim and bitter they grew, how quiet and bitter. They thought of themselves as undertakers, cutting off the limbs and crushing a huge corpse into shape so that it would fit a small coffin. I really couldn't bear those people, either because I had been one of them or had at least come dangerously close to becoming one of them. . . ." He shrugged. "I don't know . . . again.

"The nation was breaking up then; no wars or revolution, just a lot of poor, tired bastards who could see no reason for hanging together any longer. Except, of course, for the air crews that still flew. Every night, while they lasted, I could hear them coming down the valley heading for Krysale Abbey, or Iriam or the Armories or the Tyne Fortress, the Yards, Calnarith, the Wastes, the Barrens—ah, Amon! Such names we left behind us; such sad rotten names. They hung on until there was nothing more to fly, until they had bombed all the places with our names and even started in on the rim nations themselves.

"I traveled around for a while, passing myself off as an optical engineer, ship's navigator, and then an electrician until I met up with Zaccaharias and Kenrick and their crew." Cavandish brooded on this for a while, as if he had forgotten some part. "Ah yes," he said at last in mock triumph, "the prophet! One night I thought the lot of them were the biggest pack of idiots I'd seen since I left home. Then, that same day, I heard a man called Marion or something like that. I listened very hard and when my mind had snapped back into something resembling its original shape, I thought it over again, all of it."

"And you were possessed, on fire with what you had heard," VanRoark added sadly.

"You should say, I was on fire *at* what I heard. I knew then, just as Lyndir and the rest knew, not only what the prophet had meant, but what he had meant in himself.

Understand?" VanRoark did not but he was too shy to say so. "He was the world, just as surely as any man of that army; he couldn't help it, we knew that. But we also knew that the only chance for any peace we would ever have—forget the rest of the world and their blithering Abstractions—would be to go to the Meadow and die. We could see, with the appearance of this last little man and his incredible manner of speaking, the last pieces going bad. That's the bleeding thing, Amon; what the prophet said was only part of it; so many of those that listened forgot to consider the man himself and the failure of his predecessors. That's where the whole bleeding thing comes together; *that* is the end of creation they were speaking of!"

His voice had risen—again, it seemed from some other place than his mouth—with the remembered disgust and fury of that day. Now it dropped back again. "So I came to the Burn. And it seems that I must be more of the world than of the rim nations because, like the world, I could not even die; I lived, much against my will and against all the lovely plans and orders. Now I'm going home. I know that there's no home anymore; it's just a label I've given to my wandering to make it seem respectable."

And then VanRoark told Cavandish his story.

The younger man spoke, he thought, almost as Cavandish had, with a voice far and removed; there was even the rude audience of the wastes, apparently almost as pleased with his tale as it had been with Cavandish's. But the world must have become bored; as the night grew colder and the stones lost all their heat, the crackling stopped.

When the noise had diminished and his own voice was like a far sea-roaring, VanRoark became momentarily aware of his new eye; the images he saw through it blurred and redefined themselves.

Cavandish looked up when he noticed the eye twisting in and out of VanRoark's skull and the changing color of the lens as different filters dropped into place behind it. He smiled one of his strange non-smiles and explained again that VanRoark's eye was not limited to visible light now. He would develop more control, Cavandish told him, in time; but for the moment he would just have to put up with seeing the world bathed in red light when there was no moon and heavy cloud cover. The sky above him occasionally blazed with sapphire lights, a whole universe far beyond what he could see with his left eye.

VanRoark began to see that just as there were many things he could perceive beyond the simple world of light and darkness, so now could he see the creations multiplying on his arm. The images were vague and ill-formed, as they had been when he had first used the artificial eye; then, his left eye had reconstructed the images on the wire frames as he had come out of the coma: somehow they frightened him.

VanRoark stopped his narrative. Cavandish didn't display any interest in hearing the rest and, at any rate, VanRoark hardly felt like telling any more of it. The older man helped him back into his bunk and plugged the cables back into the arm.

XXI

Cavandish told him he had been out for only five days this time. It was raining heavily and the plain had turned largely to mud. He led him down through the corridor to the other end of the car and then opened a door, reached out and opened another in the car in front. They worked their way forward until they reached the control car. VanRoark could feel the humming of the engines much more clearly here; Cavandish said the bottom deck of the car held four turbines and dynamos. Current from there was carried outward and aft to electric motors buried in each of the twelve foot wheels.

The control room took up the whole forward half of the car; there was a low bench, raised in the center for the driver. In front of this raised section, a panel was fitted with a steering wheel, throttles, gauges and other things at which VanRoark's knowledge of machinery would only allow him to guess. Cavandish mounted the driver's throne and gestured that VanRoark should sit beside him.

He fooled with some of the controls and VanRoark heard the subdued wailing of the turbines rise under the floorboards. *Why?* he asked himself again. *Why does everything sound as if it comes from someplace other than its obvious source?* The sound of the turbines and now the remote jounce of the huge wheels against the desert soil, four hundred miles away. Ever since they had come upon the army, wrapped and shrouded in sea fog, he realized his senses had become more distrustful of what they reported. Perhaps if this Kenrick had given him an ear of copper and brass, then he would hear the sounds of things as they really were; but he was chilled at this thought and tried hard to listen to Cavandish, discoursing upon the history of the indisputable distant mountains (but only, VanRoark despaired, if he did not increase the magnification of his right eye).

He seemed to be right back where he had been on board the *Garnet*, with all reference points and perspectives falling away from him. This was particularly bad, for he had thought that here, in a creation of the old world or at least one of its descendants, he should have felt more secure than ever, with the steel and fiber of the old worlds riveted and welded into his own body.

The hand and eye burned on him. They felt completely normal except, of course, when his eye decided to wander off into some unknown extreme of the spectrum. It was his own mind that terrified him; it seemed to have developed a sudden talent for thinking up the most perverse observations on his new limbs to fill the spaces where the Sea and the promises of Timonias had been: How would a woman enjoy the touch of the hand inside her? Would he corrode from it? Could he rent himself out to carnivals? And when Cavandish's dead friends saw him walking alone with his arm and eye, would they come in their wrecked and rusted bombers to crush him? He asked himself if it was his own blood that lubricated the arm, or if by now his body was fed by machine oil.

Even then, on his first full day awake since he had left the Burn, these thoughts began to prey on him and he knew that he had the makings of a fine insanity. He also knew that this obsessive madness would involve a monumental hatred for Cavandish; but this was one of the things he chose to ignore.

They passed to the east, bending gradually southward, as there they could find one of the numerous fjords of the Talbight River system; they could also avoid any possible contact with Enador's remaining river monitor. Cavandish said that the one which had been anchored off the Burn had been sunk in the first few minutes of action; a cruiser had rammed her at twenty knots and her badly cast and recast armor had parted easily.

Slowly, the pebbled desert changed into rough badlands. There was only the long, rolling stone floor that marked the roots of ancient mountains; the land was split by sharp crevices that seemed to run from horizon to horizon, like the grid lines on a vast chart or spider's web. Eventually, Cavandish pointed out, the lines would become more numerous, intersecting at more points; boulders would be wrenched from the solid rock and the land would be like the desert they had just left. There were not enough small stones yet for applause to an evening's story, rather, individual cracks that sounded like artillery pieces dueling with each other.

Although Cavandish was now letting him take occasional turns at the wheel, the journey was a boring one. The land was one of unremitting sterility; the huge masses of rock did not even allow the wolf-spiders and other subterranean life which contrived to live in the desert to exist. Oddly, the two men had spoken comparatively little since their first few days together. VanRoark asked the old man as courteously as he could, if there was nothing more to talk about, if the substance of his life was so meager as to support no more conversation. Cavandish said that if VanRoark cared to put it in such a manner, then he supposed it was true; he added that there were many other things he might have talked about once, but now it would be worse than useless. Then Cavandish asked VanRoark why *he* did not offer more conversation and smiled his thin, machine-smile when VanRoark saw that he had come to view things in the same light. Talk of the prophets, Armageddon, the army, the Burn, the rim nations, his past—everything was fixed in its own meaningless death; the talk only brought pain.

But there was a thing which VanRoark had never really had; thus it could not have been lost and thus it could not truly hurt him. This thing was History; he had known of it, but Cavandish had possessed it, more than Smythe ever had, and when he spoke of the old countries, of the star-nations, and of the rim nations, now all gone or cracking into dust like the badlands around them, it hurt him tremendously.

The train had a small library, really nothing more than a jumbled collection of pornography, technical literature, and history that its previous crews had brought with them and left aboard, or simply forgotten in the chemical toilets. The history, perhaps the most incongruous section of the library, was explained by Cavandish in that, before the Burn or the failure of previous Armageddons, the rim nations had naturally had a great interest and pride in their heritage. If one must know the past to know the future, it was reasoned, then perhaps the study of past days could yield the answer to setting the world right again.

VanRoark read the old, disintegrating books, some of them of enormous antiquity, that Cavandish said had been brought back from the stars when some man's family had come home again; others were of the more popular sort, luridly illustrated but still perhaps containing some fragments of truth. He forgot his new arm and the eye that sometimes showed him the page in the reversed, red-tinted shades of infrared, the barren land, the world on which there might be nothing but the train, and submerged himself in the grand deeds and high aspirations of the past. He rediscovered the hope and grandeur that Smythe and the rim nations' planes and ships had hinted at, safely tucked away in the unreachable past, beyond even the world's immense talent for corrupting things. There the nations remained, inviolate, the sketches of their flags and devices seeding his mind for greater meanings; the few ships, the rotting, decaying merchant cruisers and destroyers that should have been sunk out of simple mercy a hundred years ago, became great fleets and navies.

From the ruined fragments of the systems he had progressively erected and then seen destroyed grew a new one, more fragile than all the rest but more awesome, for it was composed of the stuff of nightmare and legend; he learned to dream again, a thing that had not been done in his family for generations.

Cavandish saw this happening and warned him against it. "Amon," he said, his lips opened not more than a quarter of an inch, "stop this reading; stop the thinking, like I have. You must keep your mind blank or at least unformed. Let the random glories of my dead nations rattle around; that's fine. But don't let them have too much company, for they'll grow and soon you'll own them as surely as I did."

Again, as in many times in the past weeks, VanRoark did not understand what the old man was talking about and was much too respectful to ask for an elaboration on the obvious. So he read and thought and noticed that, warn as he might, Cavandish could never really bring himself to actually limit the reading.

As they moved to the southeast he could sense more and more the stirrings he had felt at Admiralty Square, with Smythe on board the *Garnet*, at the Burn, becoming the past. And late one night, when Cavandish was below in the control car, in the green instrument light, navigating the train over an ancient road, he stood atop the car gripping the forward railing. It was cold that night; the sky was clear and the half-moon turned the ragged clouds that had sprung up all around the horizon to a luminescent white. It looked as if the world around them was on fire; VanRoark wrapped one hand tighter around the railing and the other around the barrel of the repeating cannon and felt the cold fire-wind sweep around him. He owned that wind, he thought, the wind that blew out of dead, frozen burnings that had once driven men to incredible heights and then made them continue to fight against a creation that had turned on them and their Creator.

Now he owned the wind and the past and the rim nations, and the stars and the suns around which they had been founded; he owned the steel and the old hands which had worked it into such wondrous shapes, just as completely as Cavandish ever had. He breathed deeply and his wind smelled of bitter metal, cordite, papers and printer's ink.

XXII

They found the bomber two days after they had crossed the Talbight River. They were moving through what might have been a sizable forest but which was now nothing more than a collection of blackened and charred stumps. The land train shouldered them away easily but their crunching made VanRoark think of the ground he had walked upon at Brampton Hall with the ancient bones just beneath the surface. The ground was like ash; a long, dirty plume of gray and black trailed behind the train.

VanRoark was steering and it was Cavandish who spotted the line of splintered trees that marked where the plane had landed. They corrected course to the north slightly and then drove down the avenue; soon, there were deep trenches where the landing gear had dug into the soft earth.

VanRoark went into near ecstasties when he first saw the ship; now it was not something foreign, the creature of someone else's imagination, but a thing with which he felt a common heritage. So did Cavandish, even though his artificial jaw and fear of belief contrived to make it almost impossible to spot.

They approached slowly. The plane's camouflage pattern seemed to be of the usual type, molted green and tan topside and flat black on the underbelly, although the black seemed to extend far past the midline in some spots.

It was an uncommonly beautiful craft: a high T-shaped tail set at the end of a gently tapered hull; long, sharply swept wings, now drooping without the air under them, engines buried at the roots. The port gear had partially collapsed and the ship leaned to that side.

As they got closer, VanRoark could see that the ship's underside had originally been painted a light gray; the black was from the fires which had been built under her. Pieces of her crew's mutilated bodies were stuffed into the engines' air intakes and exhausts. "Our world," Cavandish murmured with his ventriloquist's voice, "and our rim nations." They circled the ship and then stopped before the shattered windscreen and nose.

"I think they were at the Burn. Rather less dignified than a death fighting by the sides of archangels and demigods." VanRoark looked at Cavandish with his right eye. "My apologies. That wasn't very funny, was it?"

They buried what they could find of the crew and cleaned some of the blood and ash from the ship. VanRoark thought of the structure he had built in his mind from his Sea musings and the old books; it did not crumble or break as these others had. He could feel it getting stronger and growing thorns; he could feel the acid welling up into his mouth. Once or twice he caught Cavandish glancing up from his work and looking at him.

VanRoark was no longer young, and the dead had none of the evasive cynicism of Smythe or Tapp; the bitterness and hatred was real now and it grew in power as he kicked the bonfire's debris away from the ship's belly.

They picked out some markers, machine guns from the waist and tail turrets, spent rocket casings, an oxygen bottle and mask, and left the next morning.

The train headed southeast again; Cavandish detached one of the empty fuel cars but elected to keep the rest for what he could find in the tanks along Blackwoods Bay. They spoke to each other hardly at all now; VanRoark even stopped his readings. Many times, Cavandish looked as if he were about to try to penetrate the screen; but he always stopped, withdrew his hand, put the book back on the shelf he had just taken it from, or simply said that the story he was about to tell was not worth hearing. Once, though, he kept on looking at VanRoark. "And now you are like me; maybe even a little worse because you have captured your history from the dreams of other men. You really don't know how we could be as miserable and as just as the army . . . and as vengeful." He touched his jaw. "And you can somehow, just as I still do, either reconcile or just ignore the grotesqueness of things like this. We see them as marvelous creations. And so they are, but you've felt the horror of them too, conjuring all sorts of dreadful fantasies around them.

"And none of this is really correct. They're not glorious or ghastly; they are only the sorry creations we were forced to throw up against the world.

"Ah, VanRoark, I could talk for the rest of my life to you, trying to explain, and you'll still drive yourself into the ground hating everything but the memory of the rim nations and what had gone before them. I've been doing that for years." He looked up and VanRoark supposed that the old man was trying to look parental, which was wrong. "You see?" he asked after a second.

"Yes, I think so," VanRoark answered and smiled, for he did at least see that Cavandish was right on one point: VanRoark hated him.

VanRoark would be almost amused at it during the few times he'd step back and listen to the undying bit of cynicism left in him. But there were few times indeed; the cynicism which had maintained itself free and clear from any real taint was now entrapped in the wires of his bitterness, trussed up like salted meat hung out to be cured and hardened.

He hated the arm this dead Kenrick had given him, and after a while he hated the life which had come with it. Why had they not allowed him to die at the Burn? Then he would have been free of this mess.

But the hatred did fill him with a satisfaction that had only been approached by his feelings of the Sea. The thorn garden made fertile by the rim nations' corpses had armored itself, even against the things which were of themselves like Cavandish and the eye and arm and the train.

XXIII

VanRoark had naturally considered killing the old man; and once again, he was more amused than appalled at himself that he could think of such an alternative as being "natural."

But it would have been pointless, beyond the simple fact that he doubted if he could do it. *Ah, then I shall let my arm do it,* he thought, *for that is hardly mine. Idiot!* came his reply. *You are not ready for thoughts like that. Monstrous thoughts like murder, fine—you've seen enough of that—but don't turn to nonsense like that to justify yourself, yet.*

He left. They were only three hundred miles to the western end of Blackwoods Bay, by Cavandish's reckoning, and VanRoark knew that the land was as hospitable as it would ever be. Winter was beginning to break up, although it should have been still immovably entrenched by the calendar.

The burned forests where they had found the bomber had once covered great tracts of the countryside; this stretch of territory, running from the southern shore of the Talbight down into the vague borders of the Old Nations, still had some semblance of normal life. Before the radiations and plagues had stunted it, the wood had been composed of ironwood trees. Their indestructible trunks, bare of limbs, towered above the blighted ash and dwarf-oak which had replaced them. Many had been burned in piebald patterns by the flash from distant bombs, some with the shadows of men or birds on them like the cliff faces outside Charhampton's submarine pens.

The train had easily smashed its way through the small trees and, by nightfall, its forty foot wake traced to the horizon. Cavandish had brought up the vehicle and coiled it around one of the ironwood trunks, this one at least three hundred feet high. VanRoark thought it looked like a huge serpent, like the one on his finger.

Now if there are signs to be fulfilled, they have been. I have seen the rockets, or at least the air ships; I have seen the serpent, the lances and the knights who held them at the Burn. And the queen? Perhaps he had known her in the old diplomatic quarter of his city; or perhaps she was Cavandish's, the one to whom the night sky had been given.

He could just club the old man and take the train; it would net him a fortune in a place like Enador or Howth. He could operate every part of it, including the automatic cannon, even if he had only a basic idea of exactly what made everything go. But it was no good; he wanted to be rid of the train just as much as he wanted to be free of his eye and arm and Cavandish.

He packed a few things the old man had given him, some food and optical tissue for his eye, and an automatic pistol with five loaded clips.

VanRoark left the coiled train several hours before dawn. His cloak was pulled tightly around him against the morning chill; he found it still astounding that his right arm should feel the cold, that the touch of the coarse fabric could warm it.

Mount Soril had come back into his mind by dawn and he moved northward, away from it, with only a vague idea that he should go to Enador. Protected by his new knowledge, he would scornfully enter into the sordid dealings of that city. *I'll become rich,* he thought, when his cynical self had become sick of the argument. And this would allow him —*to wander,* the histories said to him. *To drown yourself in pity for dead things,* the cynicism said, having lost all patience.

It took him about two more months to reach the lands of the great trading city-state. He had effectively silenced that annoying bit of himself which had been plaguing his beliefs since Admiralty Square; the thorn garden had grown to fill up his empty consciousness instead. There was no more room left for it.

He had never been through the countries of Enador before, but he thought that from the stories of its wealth and power it should have presented a more prosperous aspect than it did. Not that it differed from the usual landscapes of the world; on the contrary, only the crests on the ruins served to distinguish them from those of previous empires. He passed along the Talbight, seeing only very few small fishing craft, made of reeds; there was no indication of the surviving river monitor.

He asked the people he met in the crumbling and decimated villages if this was indeed a city of mighty Enador. It was, they would answer absently, transfixed by the blued gauntlet showing under his cloak and the swiveling tube where his right eye should have been. VanRoark then lost all interest in Enador and plunged into a fine fit of cursing against Kenrick and Cavandish and their steel and glass. If only they had just saved him, he might have passed himself off as the victim of an honorable war, if such things ever existed, or speak truthfully: that he had been maimed at the Burn in the service of God. And those that knew, those who had heard the prophets or tales of them, would nod knowingly at him, acknowledging his miserable but still gallant fate.

VanRoark purchased a brown leather eye patch at a village called Nine, and took to tying his arm against his body under his shirt.

He reached Enador's walls without discovering why her lands had come to such a deplorable state; either the people had not known or he had not gotten so far as to ask. The walls were deserted, very irregular in a city of her reputed wealth. When he saw the gates hanging open on the west wall, he correctly guessed that Enador had died quite some time ago. It was not war that had killed her, for the enemies would have been sure to have razed the city. It was not plague, for there were none of the usual sacrificial funeral pyres that would have been built outside the walls.

He could smell nothing, but this could mean that whatever had overtaken her had done its work more than a year ago; he could tell that from the condition of the surrounding lands.

It had been the lizards from the Enstrich, he finally learned. The great war between Cynibal and Ihetah-Incalam had eventually reached northward to the great swamp. The gases and explosives and fires of raiding bands, then completely beyond the original causes of the war, fighting simply because they had been fighting for years and saw no reason for stopping, had probably upset some delicate balance. Except for the Sea, the Marshes were the last great ecological system that still functioned on earth. VanRoark and Tapp had seen only the part which was still being kept alive by the Sea; inland, over the horizon, the Marshes had turned to sterile mud and dead greenery. With no more food, stopped on the south by the poisonous still-burning ruins of Cynibal and Blackwoods Bay, on the west by the equally poisonous lands of the Old Nations, most of the huge reptiles had been forced to move northward to find food. Apparently the great city of Enador had provided the reptiles with an adequate meal in the year or so since VanRoark had boarded the *Garnet* here.

There were not even the usual complement of vagrants living here now. Enador was just a depopulated ruin like Mount Soril, only a bit more grand. VanRoark walked through the city, down its few broad avenues whose fountains were now dry and commemorative pylons edged with moss, like those on the Avenue of Victories in his home city. It had not been an utter rout; a long siege and then infiltration through the sewage systems seemed most likely to VanRoark. And there had been little panic; the looting was obviously methodical and well thought out.

VanRoark sat on the steps of a temple, resting and trying to figure out what his next move should be. He was quite deep in this thought, with the usual overlay of rim world bitterness, and so did not hear the dragon stepping out of the temple and walking slowly down the broad steps toward him. He did not notice in the least until the sun flashed on the crystalline growths of its hide; even then he thought the prismatic diffractions at the limits of his vision were only caused by his right eye's rebelliousness.

It was only when it had fastened into his right arm that he really saw it. His first reaction, aside from the normal reflex of trying to jerk free, was to curse Cavandish for not endowing the arm with superhuman strength; after all, it was a machine, was it not? Why then had not the old bastard at least given him something truly exceptional?

It was no stronger than the original had been, and seemed at the moment to be capable only of conveying pain to his mind. VanRoark swung his free hand at it, but the creature only released the arm, snapped at his fist and then fastened on again.

The left hand did not report pain. VanRoark looked frantically down at it and saw that it was bleeding jewels like those which covered the lizard's hide; not entirely, though, for the priestly robes of its last meal, purple embroidered with jet and gold, were still wrapped around the creature.

A reliquary! VanRoark thought madly, a reliquary such as

those behind the altars at home, where the bones and mummified hands of saints were preserved for the faithful's veneration. It could only be that, so wondrous the creature appeared. He reached out again with his hand, but this time to caress the encrusted body and flat, armored head.

The lizard did not bother to let go this time, but slashed out with its forefeet. Small scars were dragged out along VanRoark's arm, and they too bled rubies and amethysts. More colors than had been possessed by the army ran from the treasury of his left arm and splashed over an even more fantastic array of twisting and shattering hues. Perversely, all the right arm could do was to continue to feel the pain.

But perhaps Cavandish's work had not been entirely useless; if his normal eye could see such enchantment, such incredibly crafted beauty, then his right eye might see infinitely more.

He closed his left eye and concentrated on the right, trying to force the various filters into revolving, one after the other, within the eye, trying to capture the entire spectrum in one instant.

It showed him only a lizard, about four or five feet long, not counting the barbed tail, ludicrously tangled up in some odd colored silk; the colors of its skin were dulled into a smoky, vegetable luminescence.

Angry and near tears with disgust at his artificial parts, VanRoark closed off the eye and looked at the murderous reliquary with his left. And then he thought, *Here is a fine resting place for my bones, where all the lizard-kings may come and worship the tiny, distorted images of my body that will shine in each of the jewels; just as Smythe once told me that an insect sees a thousand images, one for each of its thousand eyes. And I will rest in its belly. . . . No! I will not, because I will rot away and the reliquary will digest even my bones—and then all that will be left will be the arm and eye, and those who come to worship me will begin laughing.*

He thought of the eye, with the frayed wires that had been spliced into his brain, looking back at the world through the thousand jewel-eyes; he imagined the arm, its engravings still clean in the lizard's stomach, with only a little bone around where it had been riveted and welded onto him, making obscene gestures at the lizard-kings.

With a grating, twisted sob, he stood up and, catching the creature off balance, brought its skull down upon the sharp marble steps; and then a second time and a third until its own jewel blood came bursting out. Studded with opal now, its brains spilled out and it began to dry in the hot sun. Then, it was only garbage.

VanRoark was instantly sickened and vomited his lunch into the lizard's twitching, torn-up body. Now the swimming filigree of color was complete for his reliquary.

He turned and ran down the steps, smearing his clothes in his own food, blood and that of the reptile. He was only dimly aware that he was mad, but the awareness grew and he came to a stop before the city's harbor, much like that of his home. The double turret of Enador's remaining river monitor could be seen to the west, her hull awash, and the great batteries trained to the north and west, waiting.

VanRoark collapsed with exhaustion and disgust with himself. Once, he could not keep a single system of values and guides intact within him. Now there was only the barbed and armored construction of the rim nations and the Sea, while the surrounding person had fragmented, his various parts gone screaming off into places he could not name.

Pain was still flooding up to him from both arms; the left one no longer bled torrents of gem-sand, but only blood from scars edged with dirt and purple threads. The right arm hurt even more, the pulses surging along its length with the beating of his heart. He held it up and saw that the teeth had not even scratched it. The engravings were still as clean as he had thought they would be in the lizard's belly; the rocket still fled from the stars, and the dragon, so much grander than the one at the temple despite its lack of jewels, was still wrapped around his index finger. It was perfect, untouched, but it hurt, inexplicably, terribly.

"Oh, God!" he cried and clamped his head into his hands; the metallic click when the steel hand hit the steel eye startled him for a moment. In the rages that followed, he was too incoherent to call upon anyone, let alone God.

XXIV

He began his wandering in earnest on that day; before, even from Admiralty Square, there had been things to run from: his home, Prager, the Burn, and then Cavandish and his dead men's arm. Not that there was no longer anything of sufficient malevolence from which to run, but rather that there was no longer anything that could be called "VanRoark" who could do the running. He could run from himself: his grand, spectral set of memories of the rim nations could run from the much too human eye and arm they had left to him; his fading thoughts of life before Admiralty Square could run from the compounded desolation that had settled upon the world.

The failure of the army seemed to have removed the last props of sanity from the world, and this only increased his fragmentation. He had once worried whether he could still tell nightmare from the real world, but had given up considering that a problem since the two were often virtually indistinguishable.

Days varied appreciably in length from one to the next. The sun itself began a slight pulsation, its energy output shifting from hour to hour; his new eye allowed him to see that this pulsing was duplicated in the ultraviolet, infrared, and radio bands. He used to watch these radiations with a filter over the eye, and when he forgot what their changes meant, he thought them beautiful, like lines of smoke, stitched together with insubstantial gauze veils, drawn progressively outward along the lines of magnetic force.

He collapsed utterly around the memory-system of the rim nations, hanging whatever he could save from his ruin on its spiked armor and letting that which no longer fit trail along as best it might. He felt like the smoky trailings of energy, without will and now deprived of predictable purpose, radiating out into space from a breathing sun that appeared black, when his eye was focused so.

The madnesses came upon him more frequently now and more easily; he was not fighting them anymore. Once, he had broken twice in the same week—although normally he could count on two and a half to three months of uninterrupted sanity. An empty snail's shell, its side eroded by the coastal winds to expose its spiral patterns, had set him off; another time he'd seen an ancient road sign, where there was no road, showing the way to Mount Soril.

VanRoark knew of his vulnerability, but cared little for it; anything he might do now, and there was no reason to do anything, would be futile and meaningless. The madness was, in its way, just as safe and productive as his normal, daily life of food grubbing and speculation upon the real nature of his arm and eye. He dropped this last activity, though, after he'd broken, thinking himself to be the arm and the eye speculating on the nature of the body to which they had been chained.

The seven years that he spent blundering around the world were wanderings of the highest order, for he was more or less lost for most of that time. The varying rotational axes of the earth and perverse actions of the sun allowed him to make only the most rudimentary guesses as to his directions of travel; the sky had been useless many years before he had left home. It took him seven years to find the Sea again after he had fled southwest from Enador.

The lands he had walked upon embarrassed him before the Sea, as if the mere thought of them should infect the life that still flourished there. The flying fish and seabirds, the glowing manta-rays, shoals of silversides, and clean sand beaches, the wondrous power had not been diminished in the least by the failure of the army. True, he no longer spotted any smoke trails below the horizon; and he could never be sure if the booming report and white chalk trails which marked aircraft might be subtle products of the madnesses he had allowed himself. But here, at least, the memory of the great ships and the reflection of the planes' underbellies were still clean and uncluttered by their own wreckages. All the world was a graveyard of ruined craft and men, but only the Sea now bothered to bury them.

There was a town named Kilbrittin situated at the very

end of a peninsula in the fragmented, northern coastline of the world. It had long held the key to the old North Cape Confederation's endless fjords and harbors, and even the few probing fingers of the Sea that worked down into the territories of Raud. Like Charhampton, it was a fortress town, but there was still reason for its guns and walls to be kept in operating order: things were different in these regions, perhaps because they were so infused with the Sea, and despite the colder weather, the land was more productive. Territories of the broken Confederacy and Raud's northernmost Houses were still coherently organized and carried on a limited trade among themselves.

VanRoark thought them closer to the rim nations for this —and for the sadness that pervaded these lands. The ruins were much more orderly here: what no longer could be used was respectfully buried or disassembled; what no longer could be understood was put away to wait. Kilbrittin was fully aware it was dying and made no attempt to hide that fact from itself.

He found a strange peace here, with the storied fortresses looming above the streets everywhere, their harsh and brutal outlines softened by the winter's snow. When a seaplane landed outside the harbor to the west of the city and moored there for several days, he could feel only that peaceful remorse, without any traces of madness. He could walk down along the quays and admire the low sweep of the seaplane's lines and wings with the engines set high atop them away from the sea spray, and not remember the bomber's crew he and Cavandish had buried. He could look at the gutted hulk of an ancient cruiser being dismantled to rearm the fortresses, and not think too much of the *W. Lane* or the capital ship moored off the Burn.

He found work again in a cartography shop. People at Kilbrittin had become used to men with strange things growing on them, and his arm and eye aroused no more than some idle questions across the tavern's bar. Kilbrittin was not fully of the world, but neither was she of the rim nations, and this she also knew. She was Kilbrittin and nothing more; it was enough.

XXV

Spring had always been a very unsure thing in those latitudes and in those times; but when the first floes of broken ice began to drift seaward from the frozen rivers to the west, he left the city and began traveling south along the old coastal roads.

Remarkably, there still was a coast road. It occurred to him that through all the massive upheavals and geographical changes which had twisted the earth, the coastline had remained substantially the same. He began to think about the Sea again, and was amazed that he should now regard its teeming life with the same odd sorrow he had felt for the city of Kilbrittin. His eye allowed him to see several more levels of life in the Sea: the pale green of lichens on the wings of mantā-rays; when he switched filters he saw their cold life fade in contrast to the manta-rays, which now glowed a deep maroon. Shoals of fairy-shrimp looked like the night sky: only red instead of sapphire, in a sky of milk rather than jet.

He felt rather proud that none of this should have produced any insanity. It had been a full year since he had given himself any cause to doubt his senses. VanRoark took all this to mean that he had reached some kind of armistice with the arm and eye. At times he caught himself admiring the arm, as fascinated by its numberless engravings as he had been when Cavandish first removed the cast.

The memory of the rim nations softened within him too: so much that neither the fortresses nor the seaplane at Kilbrittin could awaken the bitter fury which had once insured their survival in his mind. *I am old,* he thought.

There was a curving headland, like the one which circled the Burn, rising above the city on the north. An arm of these hills had extended into the Sea in earlier days, forming the roadstead to her great harbor. But now most of the rocks had been eaten away and the harbor was a walled garden of cypress trees and rushes; there were a few hulks of sailing ships set in the garden at random intervals like statuary put there to give the place a synthetic charm or novelty.

The city did not appear too far different from when he had left it; even so, VanRoark camped on the headlands that night, his eye probing the silent houses and the white line of the Avenue of Victories. He could see nothing against the Sea and the surrounding rocky lands, which retained the heat of the day; the city appeared as a blurred monotone, sometimes colored red, at other times white or black.

VanRoark awoke at dawn and ate a breakfast of dried fish he had brought from Kilbrittin. He rechecked his old pistol and made sure he could reach it quickly; there were only three full magazines left.

VanRoark entered through the little Chandlers' Gate on the northern side of the city, very close to where the Goerlin River had emptied into the harbor. Old Navy Dock ran out into the mud and dust now; the rusted hulls of the tugboats and sailing launches were still tied to the dock, covered in dirt and strangler vines.

He did not go to Admiralty Square and similarly avoided the old Thurber District. His house was reasonably intact, though it had probably been vacated at least two years ago. They had left calmly, with plenty of thought, as was their manner; nothing was left behind which could not have been conceivably taken on a long journey, given horses and a wagon. There was only a smashed windowpane in his room, and the frail skeleton of the gull that had done it rested on the bare floor; its blood had stained the boards a darker shade of mahogany beneath the dust.

VanRoark had hoped he might feel an entirely sane ruefulness at his former home; but although he remembered all the things he had done in it, he could feel nothing. A touch of the fits, he mused, would at least have shown some respect for his parents.

It was still early. VanRoark moved about the sections of the city he had known, around the waterfront districts and rows of chandleries that had been given up years before he had left for the Wars. He summoned up enough courage to venture into the Thurber; the fantastic architecture the dead envoys had brought with them was eroded into even more incredible shapes by the Sea and desert winds: spires and leaning minarets, miniature temples and forts that made the southerners feel at home on the North Sea's shore; soaring, towered embassies that had ended in broken stone and mortar, left behind by their excellencies from Iannarrow and Mountjoy.

Again nothing; he could not even remember her face.

By early afternoon VanRoark had toured most of the areas he had wanted to see. Those which had been missed would have failed to stir him anyway, so he began walking along the Avenue of Victories toward the Artillery Gate.

The cathedral was about a quarter of a mile beyond the gate; he wanted to see it again, for it reminded him of Brampton Hall. The old words of Tapp's drunken song drifted back to him for the first time in years.

Mosses had grown up between the stone slabs, bordering them with green and leaving only a little stained white in the middle. Small grasses and shrubs, saltbrush, had further split up the road. Around the steps of the cathedral the vegetation died out. Aside from some shattered panels in the rose window and the windows flanking it, the huge cross-shaped building appeared virtually unchanged.

VanRoark moved slowly up the broad sweep of steps, carefully searching himself for some small swellings of memory or feeling. There was only the old awe and wonder he had always felt for so vast and magnificent a creation, and the words of Tapp's song. The mosaics of colored glass and seashell still rose within the entrance arches of the church, their saints and angels and praying men brilliant and glittering in the indirect sunlight. He wondered what might have caused the abandonment of the town and the church. Certainly not war or raiders; the gold leaf was still on the domes of the transept wings and wound around the serpentine columns before him, though a little worn away by the weather.

A single statue, he could not identify who it might represent, had shaken loose from the portico roof and lay broken off to his right. Its fellows, the compassionate popes and archangels, looked down upon it with their calm eyes of inlaid alabaster, opal and ebony, their scepters and shepherds' crooks pointed upward, their left hands gently extended downward to the smashed figure.

VanRoark felt something growing within him at last: the sorrow of Kilbrittin and her fortresses and flying boats.

He advanced into the shadowed silences, through the grills of wrought iron and to the great bronze doors, aswarm with saints and the damned. He was reminded of his arm, but there were no ships on the doors, no hunting parties or fair ladies, no dragons or knights.

Then he saw the ships again and wondered if he had suddenly slipped into one of his spells. He looked up to the vast roof of the cathedral and to the great dome, almost an eighth of a mile distant from where he stood; the whole cycle of birth, death, damnation and salvation, which was the living skin of the cathedral, was repeated, drawn together from its rambling exteriors and hidden chapels and magnified in grandeur a hundred times. All the Twelve Great Books were illustrated, the false-Armageddons from which so many saints had unwillingly walked away. There were horses, wild with the sight of battle and Heaven, running from the sacred fields, their brocaded hangings flying in a wind of amethyst and silver. There were tanks, blasted and destroyed, whose sense of defeat came from the artisans who had shaped them from pictures in old books, thinking them to have been as marvelously alive as the battle-horses, unicorns and gryfons that carried men in a spiraling path around the dome.

Part of the dome had either collapsed or been holed by a dud shell. The sunlight streamed down through it in dust so thick as to make it appear almost liquid. It joined other streams, colored from ruby to turquoise by the windows, and splashed down over the floor and rows of aircraft that sat parked upon it.

VanRoark believed all of it, until his eye got down to floor level where it should have been swept along the empty, geometrically patterned floor by the closing lines of pillars to the main altar. Instead, sitting with a peace and tranquility that was almost jarringly discordant with their appearance were three rows of big fighter aircraft; the dusty, silent torrents of colored light had turned their stained gray and olive battle paint into soft harlequins. Their high-set wings were tucked back against the hulls like sleeping birds.

Now the sorrow descended on him without any madness or confusion. Again he saw a discordance, this time in the smooth, flowing contours of the ships, with the colors from the windows—they might have been poured and shaped from their molten substance—and how they contrasted with the baroque swirlings of men and nations racing across the ceiling.

Why? Maybe they had been brought here by worshipers, but that made no sense; these were creations of such as the rim nations and therefore to be despised. Perhaps they had landed out of chance or plan in the stony summer-hard arm of the Greenbelt that passed near the city, and then taxied, their wings reverently folded and their bomb shackles briefly dipped in the holy water font, into the abandoned church for protection. *Until when for what?*

There was nothing to answer any of this.

They lifted above him as he walked forward, the first things he had ever seen that the cathedral could not overwhelm with either its size or beauty. He felt along their flanks, which were cool or warm depending upon whether they had been in shadows or colored light; he had not done that for years either.

VanRoark expected that his mind would speed up, awash and near drowning with this mystery; perversely, it slowed down and became frosted and softened with the dust of the ships.

There were no thoughts, not a single grand conception he could grasp here. He knew that a hunt for meanings or a sign would be wrong. The only fragment clear to him was just what he could see and feel.

And as he saw and touched, he could sense the menacing, thorn-armored memories of the rim nations become softened with the funereal dust, and speckled with the endless colors. Suddenly the system was not so brutal and demanding. It lost its triumphant bitterness; it only was.

The aircraft were pointed away from the altar; he was at the top of the ebon steps, his back to the great altar-block of carved crystal. The twin exhausts of each plane gaped back at him, the tops of the vertical stabilizers about level with his eyes.

VanRoark stood there, looking over their dolphin hulls as he had done with the aircraft at the Burn: the flowings of color moved across their wings, across the flattened, rotted rubber of their landing wheels.

Then he moved from the altar, over the crypt where his grandfather had been buried, and down the north aisle, between the planes and chapels. He had played in the dark, isolated chapels when a child. He would sit quietly off to the side, surrounded by cherubim or between the long, stone plaques that proclaimed the virtues of some dead bounder, and stare wonderingly at the people who would come there. They were different in his thought, for they scorned the high altar's magnificence, almost as if they wanted to pray to a lesser god than that which was represented there.

In one of the small chapels he saw the first evidence of looting; a small window had been removed and the gold inlays of the little altar had apparently been pried off.

The chapel had been built to contain a reliquary: THE HAND OF WOLFE, a plaque told him. The thieves must have been after the dust of the mummified hand because the reliquary case had been discarded under a bench.

Appropriately, the case had been shaped like a hand, but in all its other aspects it was quite unlike the ornate, usually overwrought candy boxes they used for the thigh bones and skulls of others. Maybe that was why he was able to touch it, pick it up and hold it up to the milky brown sunlight of the remaining alabaster windows, and think only briefly of the lizard and Enador; that madness had been lost among a hundred similar and a thousand more revolting ones.

The hand was hollow, to contain the saint's; its outer skin was outlined by the endless flowing strands of poured silver. It was as if someone had made a wax mold of a fine hand, strong but still suggestive of sensitivity and gentleness, and then carefully traced the molten silver over it, letting the interstices of strings melt into each other until the whole hand was not covered but defined by the spider's webbing, and the wax would have been melted away.

VanRoark noticed that while he admired it, he held it in his right hand. The reliquary hand was what the steel hand might have created if it was striving to approximate, but not duplicate, its own life—just as a man's hand had once tried to invest the steel arm with the qualities of his own.

He decided to put it into his backpack and examine it later; he walked back to the nave, ducking to miss the javelin noses of the planes.

VanRoark did not know exactly where he was going then, so he began drifting south again, along the coastal road he had traveled years ago. Then, he had been filled with a boiling, reasonably solid purpose. Now, he had only a vague conception of what he might do and where he might go, as if he could not quite reveal it to himself yet.

He left the Sea at Farnbrough Bay. There were few people along the way; a troop from Larine going to extract some tribute from what was left of New Svald was about the largest party he encountered. There were no young men seeking jeweled lizard hides.

Oddly, he found the Belt, or at least the southern portions of it, supporting some life beyond saltbrush and wolf-spiders. Small, stunted fruit trees, scarcely taller than himself, had sprung up at random intervals, where the infrequent rains had washed away enough poison to let them grow. They fed him as he crossed inland across the Belt. The perversity of the world's weather for once helped him, and an early freeze allowed him to cross the Shirka River and enter Svald.

It had taken him six years to find the Sea, but only two to find the train.

He was moving in a southeasterly direction, across the desolated Old Nations' lands, toward Blackwoods; Cavandish had said he was driving in that direction for fuel.

It was a place of wild, deeply scarred highlands and rolling swells of limestone, overlaid by an inch thick layer of spongy mosses and blown soil. Constant winds kept the few trees which had managed to sink roots into the water-rotted stone low, bending along the line of the ground like old men about to die.

The train was stopped at the bottom of a protective depression. He did not notice it at first, for the faded camouflage blended almost perfectly with the valley's spotty vegetation. Cavandish had made his camp there; a tarpaulin, speckled olive and tan like the train, had been stretched out from the left side of the first passenger car. One or two of the lines had broken from decay, and the sheet flapped roughly in the diminished wind.

A camp chair was set up against one of the car's wheels. Cavandish's corpse still sat in it. The insects and few birds of the region had trimmed most of the flesh from his bones. He sat there, quite unidentifiable as Cavandish, quite indistinguishable from any of the hundreds of corpses and skeletons VanRoark had seen in his wanderings. The skeleton's sole claim to identity was Cavandish's metal larynx and jaw; it was a tulip-shaped affair of a dull copper material, narrow where it had lain along the throat, and then expanding upward to duplicate the shape of the original jaw. There was a small oval grid where the mouth would have been; it was neatly flush-riveted to the skull—a very workmanlike job.

As VanRoark approached the skeleton he could hear it talking. Later, he would discover that the units powering the artificial speaking unit had unaccountably kept on functioning. In the absence of any coherent signals from the brain—the connective wires lay frayed and tangled inside the empty skull—the unit kept up a sporadic chatter of random sounds, sometimes joining them into a coincidental word or even a full sentence. Usually it was gibberish.

VanRoark was amused at this grotesquerie. "Even from your grave you're telling me your sorrows," he said and laughed at the skeleton; he received a garbled eruption whose closest approach to sense was satisfactorily obscene.

Then he drew back, remembering how funny he had thought Tapp's death at the Burn; and he remembered the first and most violent of the madnesses that had followed. Walking backward, afraid to take his eyes off the corpse, he lost the sound of the ventriloquist's voice under the wind and the tarpaulin's flappings.

Nothing happened; he was properly upset, of course, because finding the train meant he would have to articulate at least part of his plan: that he was going back to the Burn and then to the Meadows.

He returned to the camp and examined the body again. "Won't be able to bury you in this stuff, Cavandish," he said, feeling the jagged rock underneath the mossy ground with the toe of his boot. Cavandish said nothing. "Come on now, Cavandish. I can't leave you sitting out here on that chair talking to whoever might blunder past without being formally introduced."

There was a small burst of noise, short syllables which VanRoark's mind perversely interpreted as "Burn."

VanRoark stood up warily, speculating on how much of this he could allow his mind to play with before it would become dangerous. "All right then, if you really want to."

The parchment shreds of skin and connective tissue turned to cold sand in his arms. He almost vomited. Pushing this down and being careful not to breathe through his nose, he carried the skeleton up the ladder and into the first crew car. He found Cavandish's cabin and carefully laid him down on the bunk.

A burst of incoherencies followed him beyond the door and he made quite sure it was securely locked.

XXVI

The machine had been carefully prepared for a long wait by Cavandish. The operating manuals were set out beside the driver's throne, and a handwritten list of special quirks not covered by those manuals had been thoughtfully provided.

VanRoark took almost a week familiarizing himself with

the machine again, venturing into areas Cavandish had never shown him. He disconnected the two empty fuel cars, removed the preservative grease from critical parts and generally did what he could to put the train back into cruising condition. He uncovered the gun and took aim on a rock prominence on the northern side of the valley; the first shot landed at its base and toppled it. Intending to pick out some other targets, he found he was shaking too badly to take aim; for the first time in almost a year he felt he might go insane. The gun was hurriedly capped and hidden.

The only thing he could not get working was the train's navigational equipment. The magnetic compass was not worth repairing, considering the world's irrationality probably applied to its magnetic field too, and the rest of the equipment was utterly beyond his understanding.

He was a year moving to the west after he pulled the train out of the valley, always verging slightly to the south for fear of blundering into the Meadows without warning. Endlessly—more endlessly than when he had been on board the *Garnet*, for here there was no Sea—the distances moved under the train, the tarn gradually giving way to the blasted forest where they had buried the bomber's crew years before. VanRoark kept the speed down to what he judged a safe rate, considering the terrain. In the grasslands this was as much as twenty miles an hour, but when the forests or palisaded badlands came up he was lucky to cover five miles a day.

He avoided civilization, for he knew very well his appearance would not cause a friendly reception. The machinery of the first world and the rim nations had been despised before he had left his home the first time, and the situation had only grown worse with time.

He also began going mad again. But this was a very subtle sort of thing, which he mistook for a simple hypnosis from nonstop traveling. Then he became dimly conscious, perhaps so dimly that he could understand it only as a feeling, like the slow dropping of small crystals into a pond: very tiny, falling with a sparkling light that reflected off their endless planes, spinning to the water and leaving rings upon which waterbugs climbed as they passed—all in silence, all with infinite patience and subtlety.

Instead of wrenching violently away from the conventional world and finding himself in what had been always recognizable as a nightmare, he would feel nothing more than a giddiness and a swell within him as the wave passed, so gently as to hardly trouble the waterbugs. Then he would see the white-streaked webs of aircraft in the sky again, heading west.

The damnable thing about it was that every once in a while there really was an aircraft aloft; his right eye would always reveal that. But he deemed this trivial and therefore harmless; he found the small fictions enjoyable most of the time, and refrained from shifting his right eye into the nonvisual spectra, lest it destroy the fragile construction with which his mind had sought to amuse him.

During those long days of driving, which stretched into their fifth month with no indication he was anywhere nearer the Burn than when he had set out, he began to bring Cavandish's body up to the control cab for conversation. He knew it to be intensely morbid, but after all, the thing *did* talk and would thus protect him from his new insanity. And when it was talking, it seemed a disservice to call it "it." It, or rather he, could still be the old Cavandish at times, glaring out of hollow sockets at the storms which occasionally roiled up from the west, or late at night, again looking up (if VanRoark was disposed to place him so) at the constellations above and uttering properly mournful tones. With time, it seemed to VanRoark, Cavandish had regained much of his rare eloquence; the coherent sentences appeared with more frequency, if he listened closely enough.

Somehow none of this affected him very much; he thought it ultimately rather pleasant, going to die in the company of the dead. At times he and Cavandish would have a good laugh speculating on how VanRoark would have reacted to this on their first meeting.

VanRoark began to admit that Cavandish had not been such a bad sort after all; he could see that, now that he had gone through all the things the old man had tried to help him avoid. He explained this very carefully to Cavandish on several occasions, sometimes when they were on the move (for Cavandish spent most of the days riding in the control cab by the sixth month), or in the evening outside the train, for he hardly wanted the old man to harbor any lasting hatred for him.

Eventually VanRoark was satisfied that he had adequately apologized to Cavandish for his behavior and that the old man had forgiven him. He knew they were back on their old terms when, near sunset one evening, Cavandish suddenly started talking. His voice had become much deeper since his death, for the absence of any brain or flesh allowed the skull to resonate with the artificial larynx, like a sounding board. VanRoark looked up at the sky, just in time to see chalk-marks tracing into the western sun. It was not very high and he would see the silver craft, a glittering bit of crystal, fire-wake behind turning to strands of carded wool.

The two of them sat looking out of the control car's windows until the sun had turned the filmy trail deep pink and then red, and then black, to be lost in the night. There was a silence, and VanRoark thought of carrying the corpse back to his cabin for the night and then watching the sky for a bit longer. But Cavandish began to talk—not as clearly as he once might have, and VanRoark had to sort out a lot of extraneous gibberish—and in the end he knew Cavandish was speaking of the rim nations, and the stars that briefly had been their homes, the woman to whom he had given them, and the dreams he had dreamed when sitting in the frigid, thinly webbed eyes of bombers.

XXVII

He knew they were climbing into the highlands surrounding the Burn because, at times, he could smell the Sea and its wet, fecund life blowing over the dead sand.

They camped for the night about two miles from a rise

which might have opened down onto the Burn. VanRoark did not carry on, for he felt small, only partly unexplainable, bits of pain and fear stitching up and down his spine. He placed Cavandish back in the first crew car, and climbed atop the control car. Leaning on the cannon's shrouded barrel, he looked up into the brilliant welkin. It appeared that he might be at a very great distance in the air, looking down upon the infinite lights of the army; by shifting his right eye's spectrum sensitivity he could see the equally infinite colors the army had once possessed. Magnification brought him nebulas, torn, scattering shreds of what had been suns, their dying pennants embroidered with star-gryfons and strands of silver, like the reliquary hand he still kept with him.

He went to his cabin to get the hand, and then returned. The wrist had been trimmed down and fitted with a lock-joint; he could remove his articulated gauntlet and replace it with the hand.

There was no feeling in this limb; the coldness of its silver base reached past the insulated sockets at his wrist. But it was an indisputably beautiful thing. There was no thought of who made it; whether he had come from the stars or from Mountjoy; or of the dead saint's dust it had once protected.

It was a long hand, long and etherealized, like those of the artists who had built the cathedral; so different from the sharp, blunt form of the gauntlet-hand, which was more like ancient engraved rifles and field artillery than paintings and sculpture. He looked at the gauntlet, at its images of ships and stars and coiling dragons, and at the engraved prince, and he thought how much the noble's small hands looked like the one he had just mounted.

There were no engravings on this new hand, nothing but the hollow web-work of drawn silver. When he moved it across the star-glittering sand and mica-studded rocks, they were all within his hand. When he moved it again, he could sweep all the welkin into its interior, its stars and burning dust pennons captured like fragile birds or fireflies in its cool beauty.

More strangely than anything he had ever felt before, sorrow welled up inside him, just as the comets now danced inside the hand. He could not fathom it, not even by charging it off to madness; it remained, slowly bringing his head down into the hands of flesh and woven metal, grinding his back into the gun's breech.

He wept, at times from the sorrow, and at other times from the anger which came from not knowing where it had been born. *The purest, most beautiful thing you have known since that woman you knew in Thurber, and you cry. Idiot!*

VanRoark fell asleep there, with his left eye red and puffed shut from the tears, and the right staring with a tearless, unfocused blankness.

He did not awake until noon, and then he immediately set out for the rise; he was so eager and fearful to see what was on the other side, he forgot to bring Cavandish up to the cab to view the sight.

The wind came to him again, as it had in the valley and badlands where he had found the train; he could hear it sigh through the bullet holes in the car's skin.

Below him was the enormous depression of the Burn; its sandy topsoil was rippled and coursed over by innumerable lines, the graves of men.

The train reached the floor of the Burn, moving forward slowly; he could hear the crunching of old bones and metal under the great wheels, the same way they had snapped under his feet at Brampton Hall. This hurt him; he could feel the sadness of the previous night returning, not as close this time, but still threatening with its inexplicable sense of loss.

VanRoark brought the train across the Burn and parked it under a huge sloping wing of one of the rim nation's aircraft. Ahead of him, across the causeway ramp, was the river, substantially unchanged; beyond that was the featureless plain, only a little less desolate than the Burn, and the gun-metal mountains to the north.

Aside from the wind and the gentle slap of the surf, there was no noise. He moved fearfully, as if one wrong step would suddenly awaken all the army's ghosts and set them to their mindless, brawling life once again.

He spent the day roaming around the Burn's beaches, looking at the rusted, mutilated hulks of destroyers, the battle cruiser and tanker; he could still spot the ordered rows of field artillery secured to the deck of this last one—except along the starboard quarter forward, where the graceful flaring of her bow had been ripped outward and up like the blossom of a huge, cancerous flower.

There were about ten planes left, not counting the giant transport which now sheltered the train; most had been flattened where they were parked. But two had made it to the causeway, past the drawbridge; they sat there on their collapsed gears, still straining to lift their dead crews and cold fires to the Meadows.

VanRoark walked over the area where the army had been encamped, along the charred lines that might have been avenues where the shops and whorehouses had stood.

Brampton Hall was still there on the headlands, marking the graves of the army and rim nations. Occasionally he came upon one of the family or regimental standards that had survived the desert's heated wind and the gales that moved in from the Sea. The enameled banners of chain mail were still bright when lifted out to the sun.

Near late afternoon, though, VanRoark became bored and depressed with the Burn; it was as though only a thin cloth had been drawn over the tangled wreckage, and any move he might make would crush a skull or put a broken sword hilt through his boot. On the surface it was a fairly clean place, with just enough ruin poking through to interest one; it only sickened him to know what lay below.

He went back to the train to get some dinner from its inexhaustible stores. He also had a little wine from a keg that had been marked as Zaccaharias'.

Toward evening VanRoark felt relieved of his depression and judged himself to be fully willing to set out for the Meadows the next day. But something was needed, the beau geste he had so desired when he had left his home city.

He hit upon the idea of a dinner; many of the old histories he had read on the train had mentioned that this had often been the custom of warriors before a battle. The great halls would be strung with standards captured in past victories; the deeds of dead men would be recited to inspire the still-living; there would be singing of the company's songs with all their fine proud words of triumph edged and polished like a bayonet by the wine.

VanRoark began poking about, all the time keeping a full cup of wine with him, and soon found an irregular piece of aluminum sheeting, about five feet by fifteen. He dragged it back to the train and set it atop seven or eight oil drums he had come across on a beached landing craft. He brought up more drums, smaller ones from the hold of the same craft, and set them around the ragged table.

He sat down at the head of the table, the dried meats and synthetic bread in front of him, the wine keg at his right hand. The sun had only been up for about eight hours and, despite the fact that it should have been early summer, a few stars were already beginning to appear in the east's dark shading.

The wine had been improved by its years of waiting. VanRoark began to feel the old battle-joy of the dead warriors rising from his stomach. He remembered the bustling, professional happiness of the army.

He must have fellows, companions with whom to exchange vast lies and sing the battle songs. He looked about desperately; the only thing living, of course, was the Sea. Amethyst flashings of dolphins and marlin dancing beside the sullen wrecks and the causeway could be seen. One could hardly invite *them* to supper; anyway, aside from the practical considerations, what did they know of the affairs of men? Had they ever been scarred? Had their beautiful, fragile armor ever been torn to pieces by the bolts of archangels or fragmentation bombs?

It seemed to him that the Sea and all the life it had protected from the horror of the land was a thing of bitter mocking. For a moment the vicious humor of the ocean died within him and he looked down to watch the white surf washing against the beach, futilely trying to wash it clean again; every wave carried back a small cargo of rust and rotting bone into the dark, living peace.

Such thoughts were not for him, though. Perhaps years ago when he had sailed on the *Garnet*, or in the future when the bitterness of the rim nations had softened enough to let him feel, but not now.

Ah! Cavandish. He shouldn't be cut out of this. The old bastard was finally getting to the Meadows and any life which might still be clinging to his bones and his mechanical voice would find salvation, or at least silence. Cavandish would know so much better than the fish or their Sea, for he had certainly been scarred. The bronze jaw, eyes of glass and steel, the arm, all of these showed they had tasted their own blood, drank it in huge gouts; it meant they were human. The fish might have been hurt, but not forever; inexorably, the Sea would heal them, set them right. The calloused scars of men seemed to give them a special vision. They had seen the true nature of the world, and that knowledge had deprived them of the delightful fantasies of life forever.

VanRoark went into his own car first and put on his old automatic, a clean shirt and, after a moment of thought, the reliquary hand.

He had a hard time with all this, wrestling the skeleton out of the first crew car. Eventually he got Cavandish onto the oil drum at his right hand; the shaft of a vanished battle standard was driven into the ground and the man's skull set atop it. There was still enough connective tissue on the spine to keep him from collapsing like a child's set of jackstraws.

Cavandish was soon arrayed like the warrior he had wanted to be, or at least as VanRoark conceived him as wanting to be, with a bandolier of cartridge cases and a semi-automatic rifle taken from the control car's small armory.

The table was still relatively barren. Cavandish told VanRoark to sit down, but the wine would not let him.

Soon there were eleven more corpses in various stages of decomposition sitting around the crude table. At least, VanRoark reflected delightedly, he had gotten members of the rim nations and the army to sit down together. Ah, the comradeship of battle!

The armories of the train were almost emptied as he dressed the cadavers in anti-fragment vests, bandoliers, pistol belts, rifles with fixed bayonets. How martial they all looked with their heads propped up by metal or wooden poles;

how profoundly their gaping wounds reflected the things they had seen.

As it was nearly dark, VanRoark emptied some petrol out of the end fuel car and set blazing tins on the table. His store of synthetic bread and Zaccaharias' wine was almost gone after he had laid sufficient portions before each man.

"But then," a trooper from Kroonstadt said in a cavalier manner, "none of us will be needing food again, will we?" A small lizard briefly appeared in his right eye socket and VanRoark took this for a knowing wink. A hearty roar of approval went up from the men, army and rim nations alike.

He sighed and leaned over to Cavandish. "This is how it always should have been. Just men, together. . . ." He waited for an answer; none came.

It was night; by the third hour of darkness VanRoark was quite drunk, but he assumed that much of the trouble he had in figuring out the words to the songs had more to do with the drinking of the other men than with his own mind. Mostly, he preferred to lean back and enjoy the singing and comradely trading of insults, and perhaps an occasional aside to Cavandish. He felt quite the elder warrior, who knows he has only one last battle to fight before his courage has been justly and honorably run.

By the fourth hour of night, the pageantry of his arm had stirred to life. He almost regretted that the original hand had been left on his bunk, for he sometimes felt that it was from the star on its palm that all the hunting parties and great ships received their light. But apparently the rust-light from the petrol lamps was enough for them: he could see the waters rolling under the quick hulls of frigates and battleships, extreme clippers running before dull silver storms for harbors no bigger than the eyes of a beetle; the mounted men with their attendants on foot, their ladies riding side-saddle and their falconers at the ready; great castles and mountain fastnesses studded and plumed with flags like knights. All seemed to be somehow marching downward into the delicate wickerwork of his right hand.

And when he moved the hand, it held fire or its own cold, savage reflection on the underside of the plane's wing, the desert patterns of the land train, the clean, liquid peace of the Sea or the stars and galaxies above.

Near the end of this fourth hour he found that his hand held storm clouds along the northern horizon, turned almost white by the brilliant sky. As the clouds moved to the east and south, it began to appear as if they contained lightning. VanRoark looked closer, hardly noticing that the singing and joking had almost died away.

The clouds covered half the northern sky now and he could see they were being illuminated from below.

VanRoark got up from the table and stumbled forward a few feet. As the cloud cover climbed higher above the horizon, the vague illuminations began to play against a larger screen: green, pale blue, red, and orange burnings flared up from over the edge of the world. A particularly violent explosion lifted its roiling head above the northern mountains, turning the plain-lands and the Sea yellow-white. Seconds later, the sound and even a trace of the concussion hit them.

"Our Wars," someone whispered in the flickering darkness behind him. "Our Wars," another repeated.

He adjusted both eyes as best he could and found them reporting only garbled, distorted images; he was sure his drink-warped senses were magnifying the whole thing beyond any touch with reality. The noises were soft—he could hear the whisperings of the men over them—but they seemed ready to break his skull open. The battle's lights were plastered over the back of his head; his vision narrowed until all he could see was the burning storm cloud and a thin bordering of stars and clear sky. His mind began to spin uncontrollably. He knew that the light was dim and the noise no more than that of a light breeze—but they crashed through his eyes, turning his brain into a whorled pulp and his limbs to rubber.

"They're still going, Cavandish!" he yelled back to the old man. "The ships I saw, they were really there! The Wars are still on for us." He turned to the group. "Should we leave for them now?"

"For the Wars?" Cavandish asked coolly; the rest were silent. Aside from the pale flashings of red or orange on white bone, there was little evidence they had ever seen the Wars.

"Where else, old man?" VanRoark replied frantically. The wine took hold more firmly; as he whirled back to face the Wars he could see the ground rushing up at him. It was possible to see the individual grains of sand tremble ever so slightly from concussion.

He thudded down on his left side, unable to move his head more than a few degrees and seemingly paralyzed over the rest of his body. Before him the horizon kept increasing its blisterings of fire and cloud-shadowed light. Then he remembered what was supposed to be going on at the base of the explosions, and struggled to regain his feet; he could not.

From behind his back a new voice placed itself against the troopers' silence and the far whisperings of the Wars. VanRoark knew it belonged to none of the men he had seated at the table, but it still sounded familiar. *It is human,* he thought madly, and then asked himself why he should make this observation. *Ah, VanRoark,* he thought, for speech seemed to have temporarily deserted him too. *You must have been expecting an archangel, the guardian of the Burn's dead and Brampton Hall. But they would have no need of angels,* he told himself in answer.

"They are still on," the voice crooned, as if it had just noticed the spectacle. "Our Wars.

"Our Wars!" the voice suddenly shrieked. "Our stinking, bleeding, *bastard wars!"*

Van Roark began to place the voice, mainly in that it was, to a great extent, not a voice. Of course it depended on words now, sounds like those he could fashion in his own throat, but behind them hovered shapes, great and terrible. The play of detonating light on the back of his skull now had the shapes dancing before it, illogically seeming to cast distorted shadows of themselves over the explosions. Again, the shapes seemed to have been known to him, but they were broken and warped from what they had once been.

They had been Timonias'.

He saw the parchment structurings of creations, shredded and charred past recognition, floating inside the words, as he saw an occasional glowing of a rocket's flight in his hollow head.

But all this is impossible. I am much too drunk; soon the voice will go away and then, tomorrow, we can follow it to the Meadows.

The voice did not go away; it spoke to him, now cooler than it had been in the outburst of a moment ago. "You see them, VanRoark? The men are still coming to them; we could still see the vapor trails of aircraft, still might have seen the ships had we traveled up the coast. They're still coming, the men! And you know what that means?" There was some trace of a grating sob behind the voice, like that of the girl at Mount Soril. "It means that this, like all the others which have gone before it, isn't working! All the hopes of finally putting some sort of finish to this filthy world have been betrayed again!

"And when they have ended, and the Meadows are left for a little while before the prophets and the armies come again, some poor bastard who lived through it will have to write another *Book of Eric,* another *Survivors.* Lord, VanRoark, do you have any idea what is going on there, what must be going on . . . Lord, Lord!"

VanRoark tried to wag his head, yes, he did understand.

Now the voice was unaccountably touched with satiric malice. "Ah, you realize? Fine!

"You bleeding bastard! How could you conceive of it, with the ravings of idiots and the possessed, tales out of moldering books, and your own childish imagination? Great ships and great men, that's what you see—even after you saw how men fight and how they die, here at the Burn, even then you still see men, straight and true, neatly disposing of their odious foes.

"And besides them, you *must* see the angels, the supernatural made natural for an instant to battle on the side of Justice and Light. You see them as men, no doubt, men of huge stature, dressed in robes of light or fire and swords made of stars in their hands. You see them both walking untouched, unscarred, through the carnage of their divine purpose."

Wrong, VanRoark thought. *Once I saw them in such purity and grandeur, but then I wandered into the cathedral and saw the sterile angels and saints of the mosaics.* But he drew back from himself and acknowledged that, for a year, he had not given any thought to the Meadows outside of the hint that he was going to die there. In the company of who or what had seemed strangely irrelevant; now the literal reality of Heaven came rolling back down upon him with the concussion winds from the Meadows.

"I think," the voice resumed, "that they are much like the men: poor, beaten clowns, called out once again from what had also been promised to them as an eternal peace and sleep. I wonder if their wings can be broken and if they hang from their bodies at hideous angles; I wonder if they bleed where the jellied gasoline or sword strokes of devils strike them; I wonder if they feel pain and the endless frustration."

The voice was quiet for a second; the clouds covered a bit more than half the visible sky, or about all of VanRoark's limited field of vision. It began again, holding in it the vicious malice and groaning sorrow of a moment ago, but now touched with a growing awareness as it heard itself say things it had known, yet never admitted for a thousand years.

All through it, the shapes soared and turned, arrayed like tanners' hawks in tunics of blood-rusted barbed wire. "And do you know what all of this progressively more wretched Creation, this endless succession of abortive Meadow Wars means, beyond the fact of one more abortive ending? It mean, VanRoark, that the thing which had given life to all of this in the first place and which had conceived of all the plans is a poor, stupid, fumbling idiot just like the rest of us!

"Ah, that *is* beautiful! Think of it! The final basis for a million years of theology and a thousand years of philosophy —nothing more than a useless pile of shit! Noble minds striding the earth, putting their ascetic necks on the block in the name of something which didn't exist. Wars, evolutions, inquisitions, pain, pain: because it was part of the plan, the divinely inspired plan—so full of eternal wisdom that it sickens me now—and therefore how could it be bad?

"The marvelous conceit which must have been in it in the beginnings. The pride, the limitless power, the complete knowledge! And then, when the time came to end it, the first uneasy tremors as it became obvious that things had been created which could no longer be controlled. Time—there was a lovely thing for you, ticking like a seven-day clock from beginning to end and then politely making room for eternity—that didn't stop when it should have. It began doing things it shouldn't, just like the seasons, the air, the stars, none of them behaving as they should have!"

The sobbing currents broke through the words, riding over them like waves of polluted surf. "Oh God, VanRoark! Look at our Wars and the men who are still trying to get there, even after their own army tried to kill them. After these Wars fail, and they will, there will be another, maybe a bit more successful than this, most likely less. And after them . . . after them . . .

"Man, the only way men know they are alive in this world is because they are still bleeding! Soon, I think, even pain will be lost to us, and then there will be nothing but madness. Ah, to be alive and to have no way of telling it from death! There's a thought to start your mind moving! Carry it a step further and ask how the living will be able to tell when they have at last died!

"There'll be nothing then, nothing but a darkness filled with gigantic, colliding shapes that will crush men and then tear them apart."

VanRoark lay quietly for a long time looking at the Wars —he dared not close his eyes.

Although now largely with the voice of a man, Timonias still carried with him the power of imagery he'd had at Admiralty Square. VanRoark saw the dark colliding shapes, the torn and mangled skins of men splattering between them, their minds and organs bloody smears on the darkness.

After a while the clouds moved northward again and the detonations all but vanished to thin traces along the horizon. VanRoark wondered if the prophet was still there or if he had vanished with the burnings. "Timonias? Are you there?"

"Yes." The reply came slowly and in Cavandish's voice.

VanRoark puzzled over this for a moment. "Cavandish, are you there too?"

"I am." The same voice. "I was Timonias."

Oh, Christ-on-a-crutch, aren't the Wars and a dead prophet enough for one evening? VanRoark thought, with a curiously clear and somehow amused fraction of his brain; he had not felt that part of him speak since the first time he had been at the Burn. But it vanished quickly as the harsh light of an unexpected explosion lifted above the earth and buffeted him.

VanRoark tried to think of something to say, but he was utterly at a loss. Instead, after some few more moments of quiet, the voice spoke again. "Amon, Cavandish, the one who had come to the Burn on the train, died along with his friend Zaccaharias two weeks after we left the army."

A fumbling silence; the voice lost the bitter command it had possessed an instant before. "Look, my story, the things I told you about the rim nations and about how I used to fly as a bombardier, all that is true—except that it happened sixty years ago.

"My nation, I told you, simply began to break up. I helped it along in this, for while I was still there and flying out against the world I received . . . received . . ." The voice hesitated and fell, searching within itself to express something but not even the prophet's full voice could have explained. ". . . You *know,* Amon. I feel the way you must have felt as you walked away from hearing me. . . .

"I was given this voice and the visions to put inside it. I was shown things, oh, such beautiful, magnificent things that it makes me sick to think of them. I was filled up, you know, as if I were an empty jar holding nothing but air, and then I was full of these visions and the knowledge. For thirty years I simply moved through this world with nothing touching me on the inside or out. Then, I was . . . was so full of that lovely power that all I had to do was open my mouth and it would come tumbling and spinning out, wrapping itself around the souls of men just as it should have done, lifting their eyes to look into themselves. And then bringing them to this place.

"So I spoke the words, and I could see the things moving behind men's eyes and all of that only made me more full and more eager to see the final, glorious climax of my mission.

"Ah yes, such a climax my Army of Justice and Light and

Good and Purity and Beauty gave me. I had left my ship to walk through the camp. . . ." He stopped talking. Van-Roark could hear nothing but a barren, crackling noise, like that which usually came out of the train's radios; it reminded him of the brittle crunching of bones at Brampton Hall and underneath the Burn's dust shroud.

Something had to be remembered; Timonias went on. "I was in the camp. I was dressed in robes so fine and white that I think I could have walked at night by their light alone. I began to hear the noises that leather and metal make when they are being readied for something. It broke loose. My lovely army, turning and tearing itself to pieces, killing men from the rim nations whose families I had known!

"No, that's wrong. It just did not matter to me at that moment—until I saw them being dragged away from their machines and soaked in their own petrol, made to drink it, and having torches rammed down their throats.

"I ran through that camp, Amon, not a soul noticing my presence. I had called them there! I, Timonias! But I found that I could not speak. At the moment when my voice and knowledge were desperately needed, when nothing else but that could have stopped the army's suicide, I could not speak a word!

"I was like the Wars. They're the last place, the final move in the game, but they aren't and the game goes along, making up its own rules while the players can only look on helplessly. So I failed too. The words left me as did the visions, and I have felt only fragments of them since.

"Maybe losing my mouth had something to do with it? I caught a nice piece of phosphorus on the lower jaw and throat near the end. I would've bled to death if Cavandish and his crew hadn't picked me up.

"You really should have known them, Amon. Fantastic men, equal to the best I knew when I was still flying. They knew who I was, they *knew*, and they saw what I had done and what I had failed to do. But they stopped the bleeding and took me away. They found you later and another fellow named Johonner, but he was too badly shot up; they gave him a new heart and even some new motor parts for his brain. He died a week out.

"They gave you your arm and eye and put you to sleep to recover. They gave me a voice again, not my own, of course—I had lost that forever in my, ah, calling—but a voice. I was very angry with them at first because it possessed none of the power and wonder it once had. Before, my curses would have literally driven them insane, knocked their brains loose from their skulls; but then, all I could get out, before I learned how to work the new voice, was static and a few random words." There was a crackling silence and then metallic laughter. "Just as I am talking to you now, Amon; just like I was learning how to talk all over again—for the fourth time in my life too!" Again the quiet. "Ah, yes"—very low—"my life."

VanRoark heard the deep skidding noise of big guns with muzzle brakes, firing somewhere over the horizon. "Are you still coming with me tomorrow?" he called out after some seconds.

"No."

"But why?" VanRoark cried to the voice behind him.

"Why are you going, in whose name?"

"In my own name."

"Well, I have none now, neither Cavandish, nor Timonias, nor the first one, Arnold."

"But if only to die . . ."

"VanRoark, I am dead! I was dead the moment the special voice of Creation was given to me—as you were made dead when you heard it, as was this fine company of fighters around us, as was the army, as was Brampton Hall.

"You go to die by yourself, and your own little fragment of creation, complete whatever portion of the great plan might have been designed for you. There are worse things, you know."

VanRoark sighed heavily through his hazed world; the far-off automatic cannons sounded like a person tapping on a windowpane on a rainy morning. "I could live in this world, or even bring children into it. Do you think that would be the sin I suspect it to be, Cavandish?"

"Yes."

VanRoark lay without speaking, random thoughts shuttling through his contorted brain without seeming purpose; gradually a pattern, only fractionally perceptible to him, emerged. "Is there any way to end it, Cavandish?"

"I don't know." The voice was old and very tired.

Frustration and anger compacted inside VanRoark's throat, burning toward his head from all his limbs and eyes. "Then, Timonias! Timonias! *You* tell me, how can this agony be ended?" VanRoark began struggling to his feet; the ground spun and whirled below him; skeletal shapes, aluminum sheeting and the fire-edged horizon alternated in front of him. *"Timonias, say something! How is it to be ended?"*

The silence swallowed up the three visions, replacing them with a uniform darkness, framed only by intersecting lines of color, each thinner than a human hair.

The voice came crashing into the night, quaking with a power it had thought lost, terrified with itself and even more with what it was saying. But it really said nothing, for there were no words; it was not the same as it had been at Admiralty Square: the purity was sadly, viciously flawed by metallic grindings. The voice struggled briefly above them. Against the vanished colorings of the Wars, the inside of VanRoark's head was filled with an awful shattering of hope. All that he had seen and remembered from Admiralty Square was taken and warped beyond recognition; the plans and shapes cracked, flew apart under the brutal pressure. The brilliant colors of new suns and the golden skin mankind had worn in the beginning of the game turned to the stale, dirty maroon and rust of dried blood, the decaying white of rigorous flesh.

Behind this horror was a greater one, accompanied by a sorrow whose immensity filled his body, drowned the softened memories of the rim nations, of the great ships and the men who had sailed upon them.

A single line of stone, the causeway, was formed when all the few, isolated stringings of color came crashing together, fleeing and detesting the crumbling shapes and the sadness behind them. Even this was compressed into invisibility and VanRoark was left alone with the voice. He sensed fissures opening all along his mind and body, vainly trying to let the voice escape.

At last it did, and rushed out of him, leaving behind it

memories of a sort he had never conceived before, far beyond those of Admiralty Square, like the filthy, still-burning ash from a cremation pyre. He collapsed into the diamond earth of the Burn, fleetingly thankful that he was too exhausted to dream.

XXVIII

Around dawn, VanRoark was awake, lying where he had fallen the previous night. Even before he opened his eyes he was aware that his brain had assumed a new, fearful configuration, as if it had retreated to within the ruined fortress the memories of the rim nations had left behind; he sat in the middle of himself, shivering, and looked outward upon the inside of his brain at the things that were arranged there, of which the voice had spoken. They hung like pieces of butchered meat; their bloodied, mutilated forms were made tolerable only by the distance he had put between their knowledge and his actual consciousness.

He peered out at them for almost an hour, until he sensed the roaring upon which the butchered knowledge was hung; it was the sorrow, and the sound of it was that of the Sea. Like clods of dirt thrown upon a field of clear crystal and gem stone, the thoughts were crucified in front of him on meathooks of marlin-bills and the unicorn horns of narwhales.

The Sea was the sorrow. Just as the voice had told him, they were the same, for it was in the Sea that all lived as it should have. From the Sea, the last and strongest redoubt of God, did all the life and energy of Creation flow; the waters sparkled clean and free as he opened his eyes. The surf was still as white as it had always been; and again, as it had always done, it washed the beach clean of the poisons of the land. As one moved further from the Sea, though, the diseases would become too strong; the same chaos which had gripped the stars and the land would prevent the Sea from touching anything, from healing it or sending it to some final peace.

He had always known this about the Sea, but had never suspected it to be so literally true before the voice had told him; that was where the sadness of the ships had come from. In each contact with the land, the ships would grow older and more corrupted; the Sea could never heal them completely, and eventually they would dissolve in harbors or come to the Meadows.

VanRoark heaved himself to his feet and turned around slowly. He saw the great, wrecked aircraft and immediately the sorrow compressed around him, forcing the dreadful bits of knowledge closer to his consciousness; he knew that if he ever allowed them to truly enter his mind, he would die. They were too strong and too deep for him to tolerate without destroying himself.

The thoughts were forced away, but the sea-roaring still surrounded him. The table was still there by the control car with the skeletal warriors sitting at their places; maggots were already devouring the synthetic bread he had set before them. Sea gull defecations spotted their decaying uniforms.

Cavandish was not there, though. VanRoark moved around the area until late morning and found the skeleton half submerged in the surf near the causeway. He bent down to lift the corpse up and take it back to the train, but he heard the artificial larynx still talking and bubbling underneath the small waves. That part of him within the fortress called it a whimsical gesture to leave Cavandish there, conversing with the Sea. VanRoark wondered if Cavandish was trying to talk the Sea into giving him back his voice. He also saw that a part of him which hung outside, on the meathooks, was too terrified to touch the body.

He edged back to the train and hurriedly started up the engines. The serpentine vehicle rolled out from under the aircraft's wing and moved west along the causeway. He knew he should be heading north, across the shallow river and up into the Meadows, but that was impossible now with his knowledge.

The road was about two hundred feet wide and, once the great drawbridge had been passed, rose about fifty feet from the water's surface. It was constructed of giant blocks of stone, gray to dull olive; the wheels rolled easily over the ancient roadway.

Once, before he had ever seen the Burn, the causeway might have proved fascinating to him with its immense proportions and obvious skill of execution; now it was just there. It had always been there, just as the Sea had always been around it, giving it the power to resist the horror of the land and the air. The water sparkled bright turquoise and crystal; sailfish and marlin leaped beside the passing train with the gaiety of dying children.

The highland cliffs and Brampton Hall disappeared after an hour or two; he stared out at the limitless ribbon and the Sea, ultimately forced to become insensitive to it. Time stopped; the sun hung alongside the knowledge for endless revolutions of the train's wheels until the meaning of both was blurred and lost.

VanRoark fell further into his own isolated well; he drowsed in the summer heat, further alienating himself from any landmarks or reference points. He glanced briefly at the ruined navigation panel and concluded that it would have been of no use even if he could have understood and repaired it. Only his eye and arm of metal and copper wire remained fully awake to take the rest of him and the train westward. He had always been on the bridge, always; seconds shrank into days while the sun stayed nailed at the zenith. Only the Sea with its leaping, playful life moved at the edges of his vision.

It might have been noon when he saw the horizon, the green grasslands atop the Sea. He drove down upon them and crossed their surface. In front of him rolled a prairie much like the Greenbelt might have been when it had been alive; crab apple and dogwood orchards were spotted before him. The road continued to travel directly east (how could one tell the direction when the sun was directly overhead? VanRoark wondered).

The city came upon him gradually, beginning with some infrequent, formal gardens along the side of the road and then progressing to villas and small houses.

The battered train seemed to him ludicrously out of place

driving upon the broad avenue. VanRoark looked at the magnificent houses and gardens; their images had been suspended in his mind since last night. He knew what they had been intended for and that made it doubly tragic. For the second time—the first had been when he had looked at the aircraft—a knowledge struck much too close to him. Only with great effort was it suppressed, shoved away and hung back for detached observation.

The tree-lined street widened into a boulevard with alabaster pylons and fountains marching down its center, much like the Avenue of Victories at his home. The villas gave way to soaring buildings of gold and glass; VanRoark recognized banners and crests that he would never see upon the towers. Jade, ebony, silver, ruby, and opal met his eyes at their every turning; every precious gem or metal VanRoark had ever imagined called to his vision.

He saw other things outside himself, reflections of the images which were already within him. The twists and convolutions of the road made driving needlessly difficult. The beautiful buildings seemed to be out of plumb in the smallest, most irritating manner; cracks and imperfections in the masonry and in the mountings of the jeweled crests kept his eyes searching for the perfect surfaces he knew must be there.

Small flaws lay over all of the city like a thin, all-pervading coating of dust, infinitely maddening in that their presence was quantitatively so minor in the face of such an overpowering plan. If only he could stop the train and run out with a mortar board and file, things could be righted.

The road passed through the city and again narrowed to a tree-bordered street, flanked by pleasant villas and estates. Around noon he reached the end, a wide sweep of shallow steps flowing down to a landscaped plain, green grass and slightly stunted crab apple. Eight or ten miles from the foot of the steps VanRoark could see a line of white surf.

It should have been an exceptionally fine park, even for this land of flawed perfection, but it was not. The imperfections that had warped the city were still present, the color of the grass was too pale and the crab apple blossoms looked as if they had been made from cheap china.

None of the inadequacies that marred the city and the grasslands on either side of it were present in the Sea. As it had everywhere, it fairly screamed of perfection and life. Its colors, the white of the surf, and the turquoise that turned to blue diamond and cobalt as it got farther from the beach, were vital enough to make him laugh joyfully, and then scream when he remembered the senile, soiled creation that lay to the east of it.

He had not seen a single living thing since he had left the causeway; here, gulls and osprey soared over the coast; dolphins, marlin, and tarpon came close inshore to play, the sun shining on their clean, glistening bodies as they cleared the water and arched through the air.

VanRoark took the train past the steps and across the park to the Sea. There was a thin beach, no more than thirty feet, separating the grass from the water and he halted the vehicle in front of it.

Now the sadness was all but unbearable; it circled close about his mind, threatening to strangle it, shoving the hideous, tragic words of Timonias flat against his sanity. But these words also demanded that he not die yet, that he get up from the driver's seat and move to the arsenal at the back of the cab.

He opened the cabinet and took out a long, bolt action rifle; it was of the classic design with which men had murdered each other for several thousand years. This was not important, though; he held it balanced in the silver webwork of his right hand, feeling its cool weight, despite his knowing that the hand should have been incapable of feeling.

VanRoark fixed the bayonet, silver and lightly oiled like his hand, felt the small, solid shock as the mounting catches locked into place. The world was clouded to him now; nothing but the brilliant hues of the Sea and the shining spike of the bayonet in front of him remained in their proper place and order.

Carefully, he descended the ladder; his left eye was puffed shut from the tears, but the right continued to function, unblurred, unshut, performing as it had been intended.

He could sense a great many things flickering by his mind, behind even the overwhelming sorrow. His boots were so heavy in the sand, his left arm and eye so utterly useless. He reached the waterline, but hesitated to touch the water. Instead, he took the unloaded rifle and the bayonet, whose metallic substance owed nothing to the earth or the other things of the Sea's creation except the basic atoms of their substance.

VanRoark waited until a wave had passed and the water drawn back. *From me?* He thrust the bayonet deeply into the wet sand and retreated.

A wave slid in from the Sea and cut itself upon the metal blade.

VanRoark watched as a darkness spread outward from where the water had touched the bayonet; the surf gradually died and the surface of the ocean became as a sheet of obsidian. The turquoise shifted to cobalt and then to dull black; the fish and birds were suddenly gone from the water; the wind stopped entirely and all the world around him became silent.

The sadness dissolved around VanRoark's consciousness, releasing the knowledge of Timonias and letting it fall away with an odd grace. The Wars were over now. He knew that, for it was one of the last bits of Timonias that still hung before his mind.

The uttermost, last thought continued in front of him, and it was a mirror. It showed him that Creation was at last truly dying; by night it would be dead.

But he still lived and thought and functioned in front of the glass Sea. He looked up to notice that the sun had already dimmed perceptibly in its radiance. It was a huge thing, though, and would probably burn on for several more days.

And when it had gone, his right eye would let him see by the light of the stars. When they had vanished, when the last flickering of light had traveled its billion years to his eye, an infrared filter would let him move about.

The heat from all things would be gone too, eventually. But then perhaps some sort of echo-ranging apparatus might be rigged up by his eye and arm. . . .

Lords of the Starship

MARK S. GESTON

The ship was to be seven miles long, a third of a mile in diameter and was to have a wingspan of three and a half miles. It would take two and a half centuries to construct. Once built it would carry mankind away from a ruined world.

It was humanity's last hope : a means of escape from a world dying in its own poisonous atmosphere, peopled by mutants and monsters.

But did the starship represent salvation . . . or final victory for the dark, hideous forces of Salasar?

A Sphere Book 35p

The Jupiter Legacy

HARRY HARRISON

Bertorelli was there when the 'Pericles' returned to Earth. And he was the first to reach Commander Rand as he staggered hideously disfigured from the cabin. From that moment, Bertorelli became the front line of defence against a savage epidemic that threatened to extinguish life on Earth.

"Compulsive reading" FINANCIAL TIMES

A Sphere Book 35p

We Are Not the First

ANDREW TOMAS

The development of modern science during the course of the past 400 years is merely the rediscovery of ancient knowledge.

Atomic Theory was worked out by Democritus 2500 years before Rutherford.

Penicillin was used by the ancient Egyptians 4000 years before Fleming.

Electric batteries were used by the Babylonians 2000 years before Konig's cells.

Space travel was described by the prehistoric Chinese 4000 years before the Apollo flights.

A Sphere Book   35p

All Sphere Books are available at your bookshop or newsagent, or can be ordered from the following address:

Sphere Books, Cash Sales Department,
P.O. Box 11, Falmouth, Cornwall.

Please send cheque or postal order (no currency), and allow 7p per book to cover the cost of postage and packing in U.K., 7p per copy overseas.